PERSIA AND THE PERSIANS

By
BASILIUS L. SARMAST

First Fruits Press
Wilmore, Kentucky
c2016

Persia and the Persians.
By Basilius L. Sarmast.

First Fruits Press, ©2016

Previously published for the Asbury College Missionary Society by the
Pentecostal Publishing Co., ©1899.

ISBN: 9781621715382 (print) 9781621715399 (digital) 9781621715405 (kindle)

Digital version at http://place.asburyseminary.edu/firstfruitsheritagematerial/128/

Sarmast, Basilius L., 1869-

Persia and the Persians / by Basilius L. Sarmast. Wilmore, Kentucky : First
Fruits Press, ©2016.
xx, 197 pages, 2 leaves of plates : portraits ; 21 cm.

Reprint. Previously published: Louisville : printed for the Asbury College
Missionary Society by the Pentecostal Publishing Co., ©1899.

ISBN - 13: 9781621715382 (paperback)

1. Iran--Description and travel. 2. Islam--Iran--19th century. 3.
Christianity--Iran--19th century. 4. Missions--Iran.. I. Title. II. Asbury
College Missionary Society.

DS268 .S37 2016

Cover design by Jonathan Ramsay

asburyseminary.edu
800.2ASBURY
204 North Lexington Avenue
Wilmore, Kentucky 40390

First Fruits
THE ACADEMIC OPEN PRESS OF ASBURY SEMINARY

First Fruits Press
The Academic Open Press of Asbury Theological Seminary
204 N. Lexington Ave., Wilmore, KY 40390
859-858-2236
first.fruits@asburyseminary.edu
asbury.to/firstfruits

BASILIUS L. SARMAST.

PERSIA AND THE PERSIANS,

BASILIUS L. SARMAST, A. B., A. M.

OF OROOMIAH, PERSIA.

"And the very God of peace sanctify you wholly; and I pray God your whole spirit and soul and body be preserved blameless unto the coming of our Lord Jesus Christ."—I Thess. 5:23.

"For God so loved the world, that He gave His only begotten Son, that whosoever believeth in Him should not perish, but have everlasting life."—John 3:16.

THE ASBURY COLLEGE MISSIONARY SOCIETY

—BY—

THE PENTECOSTAL PUBLISHING CO.

1899.

Dedicatory.

ASBURY COLLEGE MISSIONARY SOCIETY;

TO

BROTHER AND SISTER HUGHES,
*Who have been father and mother to me during the last
three years;*

TO

MY DEAR WIFE,
Who has been awaiting my coming five years;

LASTLY, TO THE HOLINESS MOVEMENT, AND THE HOLI-
NESS PEOPLE, WHO WILL SEND UP THEIR PRAYERS
TO GOD IN MY BEHALF,

THIS BOOK

IS RESPECTFULLY DEDICATED BY THE AUTHOR.

PREFACE.

During my five years' stay in the United States, I have traveled over about half the country, and it has been my privilege to lecture before many religious societies of different denominations. I have told the sad story of my country, showing its needs. While the lectures have touched the hearts of thousands of God's children, yet, in the limited time allowed a speaker, I have been unable to give a satisfactory outline of the Persians and their country. Prominent men and women have asked hundreds of questions, after my lectures, concerning the present condition of Persia, the land of the Bible. Again, several books have been written by those who have made only a hasty journey through the country; and, in consequence, have greatly misrepresented Persia and the Persians.

For the above reasons, I have endeavored to give in this book a brief account of the present condition of Persia.

Further, the author availed himself of such help as he could use from Rev. S. G. Wilson's, "Persian Life and Customs"; I. M. Yonan's, "Persian Women"; M. G. Daniel's, "Modern Persia," and J. Perkins', "Residence in Persia." In these he found much that he desired to say already expressed in better English than he could command.

He would also thank the students of Asbury College for their kindly help in writing the English of his MSS.

Trusting that God, the Father of our Lord Jesus Christ, will use this work for His glory in moving the hearts of many of His children toward Persia, this book is put before the public by the author.   B. L. SARMAST.

Asbury College, Wilmore, Ky.

A Sketch of the Author's Life.

BY REV. CHAS. H. NEAL.

Basil L. Sarmast was born, June 10, 1869, in Zivig, Oroomiah State, Persia. He is the oldest of five children born to Lahchin and Shasulton Sarmast. His father was a musician and spent his life playing at theaters, shows, etc. His mother was a simple-hearted, typical country woman of the Orient.

The early influences surrounding the boy were not altogether conducive to the development of that moral character which every youth should possess. At the age of nine the father began to train young Basil in the art of his own occupation, but that good angel whom God has so often sent in the person of a good mother, prevented him from following the steps of his sire. Two years later, a missionary visited the Sarmast homestead in the interest of a school which he desired to establish in that vicinity. Sire Sarmast furnished a room for that purpose and the school was begun. When Basil was eleven years old his mother started him to the school and by that means interfered with his study of music. His advancement in his studies was rapid and he was well pleased with school life, which could not be better expressed than in his own words: "After a short time I felt happy, because I learned how to read and how to spell, and I found it was very good and interesting." After spending three years in the town school, he was sent to the Academy, completed the course, and entered college. He graduated from Oroomiah College, July 16, 1890. Having finished the collegiate course, he entered the Theological Seminary, but disbelieving the Calvinistic tenets of Presbyterian theology, quit the institution. On February 16, 1893, he was married to Nargiz Shimoon.

His early religious training was in the Nestorian church, but at the age of seventeen he was converted (Feb. 15, 1895) to God and united with the Presbyterians. Soon after his conversion, he began to feel a need of something more in his soul than what he had yet received. Of this he says: "But after my conversion I found that I needed something more than this in order that I might be a faithful servant for my Lord. I tried to get all information I could in that way from my teacher, but could do nothing." That unsatisfied longing gave him much trouble of mind and heart.

Still feeling the great need of more spiritual power, he decided to come to America in search of knowledge of the Holy Ghost of whom he had read in his Bible— especially the Pentecostal bestowment. Having spent only three months with his young wife, he started for this country and landed in New York City, September 20, 1893, without money or friends. But "the Friend that sticketh closer than a brother" provided for him. A good Baptist minister of New York gave him money and sent him to Colgate University, a Baptist school. Not finding there the experimental knowledge of the Holy Ghost that his heart so eagerly yearned for, he left the university and began lecturing and preaching in various parts of the United States. While in search of a school where he could be satisfied, he met Rev. J. W. Mitchell, of Covington, Ky., who directed him to Asbury College, Wilmore, Ky.

In his own way he tells us that when he first saw the place he said to himself, "There I shall be satisfied."

At the time of his arrival there, January 2, 1896, Mrs. Mary McGee Hall was conducting a revival in the Methodist church, preaching entire sanctification. This gospel message was what he so much needed and had so long sought after. It was not long until God powerfully sanctified him by the Holy Ghost.

For two years following, Brother Sarmast was connected with Asbury College, and all who knew him learned to love him. Always of a bright and happy disposition, he made friends wherever he went. His life was deeply pious. He had a keen sense of the right, and his interpretation of the scriptures was marvelous for one of his opportunities. The simplicity of faith and soundness in doctrine which he possessed, made him a fit vessel of the Lord to carry the glad tidings to lost souls.

May 25, 1898, he took the degree of Master of Arts from Asbury College, and July 15th set sail for his native land, where he expects to give his life in the service of God in spreading full salvation in that

time-honored country. Since his arrival there, he
has been preaching the gospel under many trying
circumstances, but his faith remains unwavering.
Persecution and famine were the first to greet him,
but He who careth for them that trust Him has kept
him thus far. Let all who read this breathe a prayer
for Sarmast in his effort to prepare a people for the
Master's coming.

CONTENTS.

INTRODUCTION.

It is an old saying that "one half of the world do not know how the other half live." This is true when limited in its application to our own immediate community and to the people with whom we come in most frequent contact. Neighbors know but little of each other and often undreamed-of conditions exist in the home nearest our own. The rich do not know how the poor man lives, nor is the poor man acquainted with the problems of the rich. Capital stops at the door of the laborer's cottage and knows nothing of the struggles and hardships and privations within. On the other hand, labor is equally ignorant of the cares and worries, the anxiety and solicitude which abide with the capitalist in his mansion and rob him of his rest. The toilers on the farm and in the shop have but little conception of the drudgery of those who live by their brains. Two sections of the same city are often as much unknown to each other as two nations. With rare exceptions the resident of Fifth Avenue knows but little more of life in the tenement districts than he does of life on the Congo.

It is impossible for us to sympathize with that which is unknown to us. Out of our ignorance of the life of those about us arise indifference and neglect and oftentimes the most bitter hatreds. Witness the conflict between capital and labor, the animosities between sections, and the prejudices between urban and rural populations. These arise not so much from a malevolent disposition as from ignorance of the other class and a consequent want of sympathy for them. If we knew each other better we would love each other more; and out of this love would spring more earnest efforts to help those with whom we have learned to sympathize. If the people of wealth would go into the humble homes of their servants, note carefully the conditions they find there, then try to work out the problem of existence on the basis of the wages they pay those servants, they would be less disposed to look upon them as mere beasts of burden,—"creatures made to serve,"—out of whom they must extort the largest amount of labor at the least possible cost. They would realize that those servants are fellow men and women, with blood and bone and brain and spirit, to be helped in their struggles and aided in their efforts to secure a more favorable environment. What seems to be heartless selfishness is sometimes only a legitimate consequence of rank ignorance concerning those who are oppressed.

If you would awaken sympathy and evoke efforts in behalf of those who are in need, information must be furnished concerning them. The people must know who they are and what are their conditions. A true picture of life in the "submerged districts" of our great cities, brought vividly before the minds of the people, will stir their philanthropy and quicken their zeal as nothing else will.

If these things be true when applied to communities, they are equally true when applied to the peoples and nations of earth. Isolation has been the fruitful source of much of the conflict and bloodshed that have marked the history of the past. Not knowing each other, the nations have not been in sympathy with each other. Wanting sympathy, they have been prone to misjudge and misunderstand. Out of misunderstandings have come hatreds and these have issued in conflict and carnage. Had these nations known each other better they would have understood each other better. With a better understanding suspicions would not have been aroused, hatreds had not existed, and peace and friendship would have held sway instead of war and national feuds. Among some of the savage tribes all strangers are enemies. China hates foreigners because for centuries she has been shut up from the outside world. If the Spanish people had known the Americans as they do now our recent conflict would not have occurred. We verily believe that if there had been as many railroads running north and south as there were east and west before our civil war, that terrible struggle between the States would never have taken place. Intercourse between the two sections would have been more frequent, the people would have known and understood each other better and would have found some other way by which to adjust the differences between them. We hail with thanksgiving every new railroad or steamship line, or canal, or cable that promises to bring the world closer together and to give the nations a better knowledge of other nations. For out of this closer touch and more perfect understanding will come greater sympathy and love and helpfulness.

The bearing of these truths upon our great missionary enterprises is apparent. A large part of the world is in the darkness of heathendom. It is the duty of the followers of Christ to "go into all the world and preach the gospel to every creature." But they do not feel the pressure of this command and move very slowly in the great work the Master has laid upon them. One thing they want in order to quicken their interest and stir their zeal is knowledge concerning the actual conditions surrounding the peoples to whom the gospel is to be sent. To generalize about "heathenism" and the "degradations of idolatry" is too indefinite. Christians want to know who these people are, how they live in their homes, what they do in their fields and shops, how they think and feel and act toward the great concerns of life and destiny. The only way they can be made to understand what heathenism means and to have an intelligent idea of the real need of the gospel in these benighted lands, is to place before them a vivid picture of the everyday life of the heathen people.

A few years ago a terrible catastrophe occurred. In one of our Eastern States, a dam which had been holding in check the waters of a lake, gave way before the pressure of the accumulated waters above.

The Conemaugh valley was swept by the raging flood, Johnstown was destroyed, and scores of helpless men, women and children perished in the awful disaster. The newspapers were full of accounts of the matter, the hearts of the people were stirred to their depths, and thousands of dollars were sent from all parts of the land for the aid of those who were left homeless and in want. Now, if the papers had contented themselves with the general statement that a dam had broken loose, a town had been destroyed, and so many people had been drowned, but little impression would have been made on the public mind. Instead of this, the whole disaster was gone over in minutest detail. Pictures, setting forth the horrors of the situation, were printed, graphic accounts were given of various incidents, showing how this and that happy family had been broken up, some escaping and some going down with the awful torrent. The distress and wretchedness and poverty of the survivors were related, and in a little while the minds of the people had before them such a vivid picture of the Johnstown horror that they wept for sympathy and were moved to do all in their power for the relief of those who survived. The committee in charge of the fund begged the people to send in no more.

This book gives the reader a picture of the everyday life of the Persians, one of the peoples who need the gospel of the Son of God. Brother Sarmast is a Persian and knows the conditions that surround his people In this book he permits us to look into Persian homes, see how the houses are built and ordered, how the people eat and sleep, and what they do. He takes us with him into the fields and market places. He tells of their social customs, of their marriages, of their funerals, of their feasts. He gives us some insight into the relations of the family, the neglect and hardships of the children, the ignorance and degradation of the women. We are then told about the religion of this people, and are shown the weakness and sinfulness of their faith. Many of these details are very vividly placed before us and we are thus led to see Persia's need of the Gospel, and our hearts are stirred by the author's appeal for help. We are quite sure that the reader will put the book aside with a more intelligent idea of what heathendom means, and a more perfect realization of the necessity there is for the good news of salvation through our Lord Jesus Christ. Brother Sarmast has quickened our zeal and made us better missionaries by increasing our knowledge of the everyday life of Persia.

As to the author himself, we had considerable acquaintance with him during his stay in America. We have had him in our home and heard him preach and lecture from our pulpit, and we feel that we are better for it. We regard him as a good man and believe he is specially called and qualified of God for a great work in his native land. The fact that he came to America in search of the Holy Ghost and to get information concerning that marvelous filling

with the Spirit described in the second of Acts,
is an indication of the earnestness of the man and
the strength of his conviction. When he arrived
at Asbury College and was asked by the President
what he wanted, he replied, "I want to learn how to
tell poor Persian about Jesus, and to understand the
second of Acts." When he received the blessing of
entire sanctification a few days later, his longing
soul was satisfied and he at once began to tell others
of the wonderful filling. The fact that he has
already had so many conversions under his ministry
since his return to his home is proof that he also
learned "how to tell poor Persian about Jesus."

Brother Sarmast is a man of fine intellect. When
he was licensed as a preacher of the Methodist Epis-
copal Church, South, it was our privilege to examine
him on the doctrines of the Church. So clear was his
understanding of these doctrines and so forcible was
his way of putting them that we were compelled to
give him the highest grade in a very large class. He
is also a man of strong convictions and has the cour-
aeg to stand by them. After associating with him we
felt that God was with the man and would use him
in the great work to which he has consecrated his life.

The reader will please to suffer a word concerning
the difficulties under which this volume has been
edited and put through the press. Brother Sarmast
left America sometime before his manuscript came
into our hands. He was a foreigner, had been in
America only a few years, and of course his thinking

was done in Persian, then translated into English.
By the help of some of the students of Asbury College his manuscript was prepared for the printer.
In editing this manuscript, we altered it in as few places as possible, wishing to preserve the style of the author and to let him tell his story in his own way. However, we met with many difficulties. There were many names that were altogether unfamiliar to us, some of them almost unpronounceable and of very uncertain spelling. Bringing these names over into the English by the aid of different students, who were not thoroughly conversant with the subject, and who had to depend largely on the sound for their idea of how the word should be spelled, has naturally led to considerable confusion. We have not always found it possible to verify the spelling of these words, and it is very probable that some discrepancies will be found. Had we been able to communicate with Brother Sarmast, all these difficulties would have been cleared up, but under the ˙circumstances the editor must ask the reader's indulgence at this point.

Brother Sarmast is now in Persia, preaching the good news of a full and free salvation to the Persian people. God is honoring his ministry by saving souls through his instrumentality. Helpers are being raised up, a church has been gathered, and the work is taking deep root in that needy soil. Let every reader pray earnestly for this man of God, that he may constantly be filled with the Holy Ghost and used in the redemption of his beloved land.

W. E. ARNOLD.

Persia and the Persians.

CHAPTER I.

General Features of Persia.

In ages past, Persia was the home of heroes and the scene of great historic events; the land of Oriental splendor and beauty. Bards of all nations have vied with each other in singing of the bravery of her sons, and the beauty of her daughters. The names of great kings, Cyrus, Darius, and others, are engraved in ever-living letters in her history.

At one time Persia claimed to be the greatest nation in the world, but at the present time would suffer in comparison with many others. Still, her natural beauty remains untarnished; and, though much reduced in territory, she has yet a broad domain extending seven hundred miles from east to west, and nine hundred miles from north to south, containing 628,000 square miles. This is three times as much as France or Germany; or, equal to France, Germany, Great Britain and Ireland combined; or to that part of United States lying east of the Mississippi, and north of the Tennessee. It is divided into thirteen States as follows: Mazandaran, Astrabad, Adarbaijan, Kurdistan, Luristan, Khuzistan, Faristan, Laristan,

Karman, with Mogistan, Gilan, Irakestan, the Capital of the State where the king resides, and Khurasan, which is the largest State, and is covered with desert. Geographically, Persia lies between 26 degrees and 40 degrees north latitude, and between 44 degrees and 59 degrees east longitude, and its population is estimated at about 12,000,000. These are composed of different nationalities; of the Kurds 980,000; Arabs 600,000; Jews 50,000; Nestorians 100,000; Armenians 50,000; Zoroastrians 35,000; the remainder are Mohammedans.

The ancient name of Persia is Elam, which dates her history at least 2,000 B. C., and derives its name from Elam, the son of Shem. Some learned men hold that as early as the time of Abraham there was an organized government, the king being King Chedarlaomer, the king of Elam (Gen. 14:1). This opinion is confirmed by the fact that Elam is the real name of Persia, the name Iram having been applied by the modern Persians. Other names are Ajam [clown], and Ajamistan, or clown land, and Iranloo, or Iranlee, and Pars, or Parsee, from which the Europeans derive the name Persia.

Persia is dotted with many great and high mountains, some as high as 18,600 feet, interspersed with beautiful valleys, flowing fountains and running streams of pure water. The climate of Persia varies much according to the locality. In the Caspian provinces, where the rain is frequent, it is hot and unhealthy for the greater part of the year; in the table-lands it is intensely cold in winter, though hot in summer. The central plateau has a delightful climate, its atmosphere having been pronounced remarkably above that of all other countries for dryness and purity. The city of Oroomiah has an excellent climate, the heat being moderated by mountain breezes, which purify the unhealthful air and make the nights delightful. The southern part of Persia has a hot climate, but the northern and the western portions have the best climate in the world.

Soil and Products.

The cultivated portions of Persia, where there is a good rainfall and where the land can be irrigated, are rich and productive. It is only necessary to tickle the soil with a plough and it will laugh into the harvest. The best wheat in the world grows in Persia. Other products are rice, barley, opium, tobacco, sugar-cane, cotton, etc. Vineyards are plentiful. The most luscious fruits are grapes, peaches, apples, pears, muskmelons, watermelons and plums, the equal of which I have not found in all my travels. Grapevines are abundant, and the Persian grapes are not only of a good flavor, but the wines made from them by the Jews and Armenians are known as the best in the world. The wines of the Shiraz are celebrated in Eastern poetry. Mulberries and silk also, are famous Persian products; while the finest perfumes are made from the countless varieties of roses with which the land is carpeted.

Persia has long been known as the flower land of the world; for in the spring-time the country is covered with different colored flowers, and looks like the clear sky at midnight. Among these flowers are many kinds of roses, also marigolds, hollyhocks, narcissuses, tulips, tube-roses, white lilies, asters, and violets. Like fruits and flowers, Persia produces the best of all the different kinds of vegetables.

Domestic and Wild Animals.

The domestic animals are horses, camels, mules, asses, buffaloes, sheep, goats, oxen, cows, dogs, cats, etc. The wild animals are lions, tigers, leopards, wolves, jackals, foxes, boars, wild sheep, wild asses, and wild cats. Among the domestic animals, the horse, the camel, and the buffalo hold the first place. The farmers use the buffalo for plowing and general work. The Persian horses are the finest in the world. Not much manufacturing is done in Persia, but Persian rugs, shawls, and carpets are the finest that can be found anywhere. They are made by hand by women. Some of these rugs, shawls, and carpets have been sold in some countries for as much as $8,000 or $10,000.

Administration.

The Shah is regarded as vicegerent of the Prophet, and as such, claims implicit obedience so long as his commands do not conflict with the Koran and the Sacred law. The Shah is an absolute monarch; he appoints governors for each of the thirteen States. Taxation is very heavy; the burden of the taxes falling upon the Jew and the Christian. Punishments are often inflicted publicly to deter from crime. Several times I have seen people beheaded, and their headless bodies lying open to the gaze of all in the public square. I have seen some men without ears; and others without hands; and still others without limbs; all of which is the result of some crime committed in the past. Torture, including the bastinado, and even worse penalties, is resorted to, to compel confession of crime.

Houses.

There are three classes of people in Persia. Each class has its own peculiar house, according to its wealth and standing in society. The first visible part of a first-class house from the street is a high, thick wall that encircles the whole lot. Through this there is only one entrance, a large gate made of heavy, hard wood, and studded with big-headed iron nails. This gate is kept closed all the time, and anybody desiring to go in would have to knock hard in order to call the family, who, in most cases, live in some distant part of the premises. Walking along the street one can easily tell the official houses, because they have always a dozen or more men guarding the gate. These guards eat, sleep, and live in the small rooms opening into the gateway at each side.

No neighbor is allowed to build his house higher than the mud walls, or if he does, he is not permitted to open any window, not the least opening, into his neighbor's yard which could make it possible for the neighbor to look in upon his wives. Entering through the gate, the interior will show the house constructed around a court or garden.

The first apartment we come to is called "beroon," or the men's apartment. Here the head of the family during the day commands his servants, transacts his business, and receives his callers. He comes to this apartment by sunrise, having previously had his cup of coffee or tea, and his prayers. And here he stays until his dinner hour, which is twilight.

The second part of the house is called "anderoon," which is exclusively for women and children, and is also called *"harem,"* "forbidden place," a word corresponding with *zenana* or *seraglio.* The women live here all their lives, seldom going out for recreation or a breath of fresh air. No one would venture to go into this apartment. If a man by mistake or unwittingly should make his way toward the "forbidden place," he would be quickly met by the guardians and eunuchs, crying loudly, "Women, away!" And the man, with breathless haste, would make his way back, while the women would begin at once to conceal their persons with the veil.

The custom of secluding the women and watching them so carefully has come down from long generations. The kings in ancient days, in order to exhibit greater state and to preserve a pure lineage, first introduced the custom into the country, and it was gradually adopted, in some form, by all classes except the wandering nomads.

The inner walls of the houses fronting on the court are of sun-dried red brick or stone. They are painted in the real Persian figures and in many different colors, thus making a picturesque scene for the eye. However, they are seldom seen by any except those who live within them, as few people ever venture inside the walls even on business.

The rooms are long in shape, with high ceilings. The walls are always very thick, not only in order to be strong enough to sustain the heavy roof, but also to leave space in the depth for takchas, or open closets, which have to answer for wardrobes.

The roof is always flat, made by putting large beams of poplar across from wall to wall, about two feet apart; then planks and cheap matting; then earth, beaten or packed down hard; and then a kind of plaster mixed with straw on the top, from which the rain drains off to pipes around the sides.

The windows are only on the side of the house looking toward the garden or court. Some of them are very richly ornamented with fancy wood-work and small-paned stained glass.

The rooms in the harem are all beautifully decorated within. The ceiling and walls are stuccoed in honeycomb patterns, some in pure white, others del-

icately tinted. Often small mirrors are inlaid to add
to the beauty. They are elegantly carpeted in Persian style; that is, with a large center-piece and two
kenaras, or side strips, and a head piece at the side
furthest from the door. The finest rugs are manu-
factured at Sinnah, Hammadan, and Yezd; and are
very different from those often sold in the American
market as genuine. The real Persian rugs have a
thick, soft fur, in rich, unfading colors of a shimmer-
ing brightness. They are both pleasant to look at
and comfortable to sit on. It is the fashion at certain seasons to cover the rugs with a white cotton
cloth, called "Rue Parsh" [the face of the carpet].
This is done by almost everybody, partly for change
and partly for the protection of the rugs. There is
not a chair or table in any of these rooms. The Persian women proper sitting on the floor rather than a
chair, and there is nothing about their garments to
make it uncomfortable for them. And if they desire
anything in addition to the rugs, they have cushions.

The Persians are not particular about having separate rooms for everything, although if they so desired they have a sufficient number of rooms. They
prefer to eat, sit and sleep in the same room. There
is no difficulty in doing this, as they have no
bedsteads to occupy the space of the room. The
bedding during the day is folded together in a calico
sheet, and rolled up against the wall so that it can be
used like the back of a sofa, and in the evening is
spread out again. Some luxuriant pillows, made

long and round, are placed around the rest of the
walls and make quite comfortable seats nearly all
around the room.   So that there is not much need to
pity them for having to sit on the floor.

Around the walls, just about three feet from the
ceiling, is a row of shelves, and upon them will be
found many variously colored bottles, containing the
most delicious Attar of Roses and many other perfumes.   Attar of Roses was first made in Persia.

The best part of every home is the large yard attached to it.   In this particular they are ahead of
the Americans.   The windows all open on the court,
which is nothing more nor less than a luxuriant garden, full of all kinds of roses, vines, and shrubbery
with shade and fruit trees planted in rows, forming
long avenues across the yard.   In the center of this
court there are one or two small lakes, full of many
colored fish.   The rills from a fountain ripple un-
ceasingly over the paving stones, giving refreshment
to the flowers and trees planted upon their banks.

Here the women sit upon their soft divans during
the heated days of the summer and listen to the mur-
mur of the waters, mingling with the sweet song of
the nightingale, while breathing the air laden with
the sweet perfume from the roses.   However pleasant this may seem, it is their all; here they must stay
summer and winter, year after year, until the last
pulse has beaten.   We have a saying in Persia which
describes the condition of these women: "The bird
never feels at home in a cage, even if it be of gold."

The second-class houses belong to the merchants and business men, differing from the first only in being smaller, having fewer rooms, etc.

The third-class houses belong to the farmer and the day-laborer. In these we find a vast difference. This class of people live exclusively in the villages and small country communities. Their homes are made almost entirely of mud, in a simple, unattractive manner, without any brick at all. The soil is moistened into mud and worked to a proper consistency by the feet of men and animals. Piece by piece it is handed to the mason who lays it by hand, until it reaches a height of four feet and is three feet thick, the invariable custom of the Persian builder. This is allowed a few days for hardening when another layer of similar height is added. This is continued until the house is completed. In most buildings, the gateway opens immediately into the house from the street, few having separate walls around them. The outer walls of the houses are so rough that the birds find many nooks and corners in which to build their nests. The main part of the house is a large, square room. It has no windows except four small, unglazed openings, two of which are in the roof and have to serve as chimneys also. Even in the middle of the day there is not sufficient light. There is only one entrance to this room, and this entrance is very low and narrow, so much so that often a man must bend his body to be able to go through. A lady missionary once said in regard to these houses: "Future archæologists, studying the ruins of these houses, may conclude from the doors that they were built for a race of dwarfs." One side of the room is carpeted with a few cheap rugs, carpeting, or matting for the sitting of the whole family, for there is no harem or separate apartment for the women in these houses. They all live together. Consequently their women are not quite so strictly secluded and guarded as those of the upper class. However, if any stranger comes in, the women must at once conceal their persons and go to the opposite end of the house.

At one end of this same large room is the *tandoor*, which takes the place of the cooking stove and the heater, too. It is circular, narrowing somewhat at the top and the bottom; it is about four feet deep and two and a half in diameter, and has a flue leading from the outside to the bottom. The inside is smoothly lined with clay. Over this is the *Kursi*, a skeleton frame of wood like an inverted table, from four to six feet square, covered with a thick cotton quilt, which extends four or five feet beyond it. Cushions are placed under this, and here the women huddle all day; and, in some places, the whole family all night, by this means keeping comfortably warm. Every morning the fire is made and kept burning for about two hours; and, as there are no chimneys in the room, it is, by this time, well filled with smoke, which gradually finds its way out through the small openings in the roof. The men can go out and escape

this annoyance, but the poor women must stay and
endure it while they cook and attend to other duties.
In consequence they suffer much from sore eyes.
The words of the Proverbs are illustrative here: "As
smoke to the eyes," etc. Thus, instead of beautiful,
smooth plastering, and handsome hangings, the
whole ceiling, as well as the rough walls, is black
with smoke and soot.

The furniture is very simple. A few mirrors in
the walls, some bottles and earthen vessels on the
shelves, with many bundles of bedding heaped one
over another on one side. These when spread at night
nearly cover the floor, as this is the sleeping room as
well as dining room and kitchen of the family. In
summer they spread their beds on the large flat roofs,
which are more comfortable than the crowded room
beneath. "Let him that is on the housetop, not come
down to take anything out of his house." (Matt. 24:17).

These houses have only a dirt floor and become
very damp in winter, especially when the rain pours
in through the openings in the roof, even though they
catch all the water they can in vessels set for the
purpose.

Attached to this room is generally a smaller room
used for storing winter provisions, etc. At some little
distance from the house is the stable and barn, full of
hay and straw for the cattle.

This completes the house of the poorer Persian
family. Among the poorest and among the mount-
aineers, the one large room which we have already

described is the whole house. One corner will be used for sheep, cows, chickens, and goats; another for the packing room; and the center for the parlor and bed-room, with the kitchen off to one side. It must have taken a great deal of grace and love to have enabled Miss Fidelia Fiske to spend so many days in such houses that she might teach and carry the gospel to these, the most ignorant women on earth. As you may well imagine the filth in such houses is beyond description.

Cooking.

The oven (tannoor,) consists of a circular hole in the earth, about three feet deep and perhaps two in width at the top and three at the bottom, with a flue entering it at the bottom to convey air to the fire. This hole is internally coated with clay which soon hardens into tile. The bread is drawn out into cakes from two to three feet long, eight or ten inches wide, and of scarcely the thickness of a common dining plate. It assumes this shape almost in a moment by the wonderful deftness of the matron, who simply tosses a piece of dough from hand to hand. Thus drawn out like a membrane, it is placed upon a cushion and stuck upon the side of the oven, where it attaches and crisps in a few seconds, and another as quickly made ready, succeeds to the same place. This thin bread soon dries and may long be preserved. However, except in case of journeys, it is usually baked every day and eaten while fresh. Thicker pieces very soon become heavy and unpalatable.

Bread in Persia is always leavened by a small piece
of dough preserved from day to day. The oven is
heated only once a day, for baking and cooking.
The holes in the roof being closed as soon as the
smoke passes out, the warmth being retained by the
framework and quilt as previously described, a single
firing suffices for twenty-four hours. The whole family, or rather the household, consisting of three, four,
or five generations as the case may be, and commonly
not less than twelve, fifteen, or more individuals, en-
compass the *tandoor* with their feet under the quilt.
At night they spread their couches around it, forming
a circle by placing their feet near the fire while their
heads radiate from it, and thus they sleep.

Oroomiah.

"Home, home, sweet home!
There is no place like home!"

The district of Oroomiah is in the western part of
Adarbaijan, the northern portion of Persia. It consists of a magnificent plain, situated at the eastern
base of the Kurdish mountains, extending from them
to the beautiful lake of the same name. The lake of
Oroomiah is about eighty miles in length and thirty
in breadth, in direction lying a little to the west of
north and east of south. Its waters are very salty,
perhaps as much so as the waters of the Dead Sea.
No fish are found in it; but fowl, particularly the duck
and flamingo, frequent it in great numbers. The
plain of Oroomiah is about forty miles in length,

lying upon the central section of the lake; and in its broadest part, is about twenty miles wide. Imposing spurs of the Kurdish mountains sweep down quite to the waters of the lake, at the extremities of the plain, enclosing it like a vast amphitheater. This great plain, with the adjacent declivities of the mountains, comprising an area of about six hundred square miles, contains at least four hundred villages. It is watered by three considerable rivers, besides many smaller streams. Its soil is extremely fertile, and is under high cultivation. Its staple productions are wheat, rice, cotton, tobacco, and the grape-vine. It also abounds in a great variety of fruits. Besides its ten or twelve species of the grape, it yields cherries, apricots, apples, pears, quinces, peaches, plums, melons, nuts, etc., in most ample abundance. Such is the number of trees and orchards, planted along the water courses in all parts of the plain, that it has the appearance of an American forest.

About twelve miles back from the lake, and about two miles from the mountains, is the *city* of Oroomiah. It is the ancient Thebarma, the birth-place, as tradition says, of Zoroaster, the founder of the ancient sect of fire-worshippers; a tradition which is rendered more credible from the fact that there are on different parts of the plain, several artificial mounds, each covering an acre or more, and rising to a height of fifty to seventy feet. These seem to be vast piles of ashes that accumulated during the lapse of centuries, under the "perpetual fires" before which the people paid their adoration.

Oroomiah is nearly four miles in circumference. Like other cities of Persia, it is surrounded by a mud wall and a ditch; and most of its houses are built of unburnt brick. Its markets are good for that country; its streets are wider than are common in Eastern cities; and it has a very agreeable air of comfort, owing to the great number of shade trees interspersed among the houses.

From elevations back of the city, the beholder, as he looks down upon the gardens directly below him, —and then, upon the city, half buried in shrubbery, —and next, over the vast plain, studded with its hundreds of villages, verdant with thousands of orchards and hedges of poplars, willows, and sycamores, gleaming with almost illimitable fields, waving a golden harvest,—upon its flowing streams, and, farther still, upon the azure bosom of the placid lake, beaming and sparkling under the brilliancy of the pure Persian sky like an immense mirror,—and finally upon the blue mountains, far in the distance beyond the lake,—one of the lovliest and grandest specimens of natural scenery is spread out before him, that was ever presented to the eye of man.

The climate of Oroomiah is one of the finest in the world. A country so charming,—so bright under the effulgence of its clear heavens and grateful with the thrifty growth of its abundant crops, presents to the eye much of the aspect of an Eden.

The most interesting remnant of antiquity, in Oroomiah, is an immense mosque—the only one in the city. It is surmounted with a dome and cupola, and was once a Christian church. It is an arched structure, finely built of brick and lime. The upper portions have been rebuilt, but the lower walls of the main part appear to have belonged to the original building and bear marks of considerable antiquity. Without the city, about a quarter of a mile from the wall on the southern side, is an ancient cylindrical tower, perhaps fifty feet high, the origin of which is unknown. On its upper part are figures, which, however, are not sufficiently distinct to enable one to determine whether they are written characters, or merely ornamental carvings. The tumuli of the fire-worshippers on the plain will be noticed elsewhere.

On every side of the city are gardens of vast extent, surrounded and interspersed with shade trees of such size and number as to give the whole region much the appearance of a great forest. Of the inhabitants about four thousand are Jews; two thousand five hundred, Nestorians—the mass of Nestorians residing in the villages—and the rest are Mohammedans. There are a few Armenians in the city and the province. The city within has a venerable and rather inviting appearance. It has much broader streets, more shade trees and gardens, and a greater air of general comfort, than most other cities which I have seen in the world.

The Costume.

The costumes of the Persians are very interesting. The men invariably wear an under starched shirt of cotton, seamed with silk. In Southern Persia these shirts are elaborately embroidered about the neck, fastening in front with a flap having two small buttons or knots at the left shoulder. It has no collar and the sleeves are loose. The lower class of people prefer dark blue, but the higher classes always wear white.

Then comes the *Arkalik*, generally of quilted chintz or print. This is a close fitting garment with a low collar and tight sleeves and reaches as low as the knees. Next to this is the *Kulajah* (or coat), in some parts of Persia called *Gemah*. This is made of Cashmere or Karman Shawl [silk], and like the "arkalik" is open in the front and shows the shirt. It has a small standing collar, and is double breasted having a pocket hole in either side to give access to the pockets which are always in the "arkalik." The length of the "Kulajah" is a little more than that of the "arkalik."

The "Aba," a camels hair cloak of the Arab, is worn by travelers, priests, and horse traders; the "Kamarchand," a girdle, is also characteristic of class, and is made of muslin, shawl, or cotton cloth.

The entire head is generally shaved, but sometimes only the crown; again some shave all but the crown allowing a growth there something like the Chinese "pig-tail." This is called a "Kakul," and is often two feet long. The wearers of these consider them as life lines, for they believe that Mohammed will reach down from heaven, grasp the "Kakul," and land them safe in the portals of glory, consequently great care is taken of the "Kakul."

The costume of the women has changed considerably in the last century. The head is covered with a "Charkodd," a large square of embroidered silk or cotton, folded so as to display the corners, and fastened under the chin by a broach. An ornament in the form of a jeweled feather, is often worn on the side of the head, while the hair on the front of the head, cut on a level with the mouth is brought up in love-locks on either cheek. Beneath the "Charkodd" is generally a small kerchief of a dark material, only the edges of which are visible. The ends of the "Charkodd" cover the shoulders. A profusion of solid gold jewelry is worn, silver being worn only by the poorer class. Necklaces, bracelets, and chains, with scent caskets attached, are much prized. The arms are covered with clanking glass bangles, called "alangu."

The face, on important occasions, is usually much painted, the color being very freely applied, the cheek being as much riddled as a clown's, and the neck smeared with white, while the eye-lashes are worked round with "surmah." This is supposed to be beneficial to the eyes, and nearly all the women use it. The hair, though hidden by the "Charkodd," is plaited into innumerable little braids of great length.

The hair of the Persian lady is very luxuriant,

and is never cut; it is nearly always dyed red with senna. Fair hair is not esteemed. Blue eyes are not uncommon, but brown ones are the rule. A full moon face is much admired and a dark complexion, termed "namak" (soft), is the highest national idea of beauty.

A very short jacket, quite open in front, having tight sleeves, is worn, ornamented with metal buttons. In the winter a short jacket of white cotton is used, also tiny slippers with high heels. The rest of the costume is composed of the "tumlun," or "shalmar," a short skirt of great width, held by a draw-string; the outer garment is generally of silk, while beneath are innumerable other garments of the same shape. The garments are very short among women of fashion, covering only the thigh. Leg coverings are worn, having been introduced in ancient times. The Persian ladies always wear them.

Persian Characteristics.

The character of the Persian is that of an easy-going man, with a wish to make things pleasant generally. They are very hospitable and obliging, and especially well disposed to the foreigner. Their home virtues are many. They are very kind and indulgent to their children. The respect of a son to his parents is excessive, developed to a high degree, especially to the father, in whose presence he will rarely sit, and whom he is in the habit of addressing and speaking of as *master.*

The mother is always the most important member
of the household, and the grandmother is treated
with veneration. The presence of a mother-in-law is
courted by the son-in-law.

Persians are clean in their habits, washing themselves and their garments frequently. The Persian
desires to make the best appearance possible, and so
is very neat in his dress.

Cruelty is not a Persian vice; but torture and
punishment of unusual and painful nature are part
of their judicial system. A man is seldom imprisoned
for more than twelve months, the rule being that there
is a general jail delivery at the new year.

The close adherence to ceremony and etiquette,
the readiness to adopt foreign habits, together with
the capacity for using, and the law of receiving, the
grossest forms of flattery, which in the days of Herodotus were found to be the notable feature of national
character, are still to be seen in Persia in the nineteenth century.

Government.

Persia is divided into thirteen States. The king
appoints a governor over each State. This governor
appoints the mayor over each city within his territory. This office is not awarded on the basis of education, ability or worthiness, but is given to the man
who will pay the most money, provided his ancestry
is fairly good. Many mayors of cities are related to
the royal family. These offices are limited to terms

of one year, but many times a mayor is removed before his time is out; the subjects may complain, or
some person may bid more money for the office.
When a man is appointed mayor of a city, the lords
of that city, accompanied by soldiers, will go three
miles out of the city to meet the new official. He is
greeted with discharges of artillery. The lords ride
on very fine Arabian horses, with gold bitted bridles,
and escort the mayor into the city. The new governor of the city admires the fine horses of his lords,
and sometimes covets some fine steed, and before his
term expires finds the way to get possession of it by
helping the lord out of some trouble. If the new
mayor is a prince, all persons confined in the city
jail are taken before him as he enters the city. This
is to signify that, as a member of the royal family, he
has the authority to behead them. The third day
after the new mayor arrives, it is the custom for the
lords and counts to visit him with presents of money,
golden articles, Arabian horses, etc.

A mayor has from one hundred to three hundred
servants. He pays them no salary. Some become
his servants for the name, some from fear, and others
from choice. Most of these servants get their living
from fines and bribes. Some of them are detailed to
settle quarrels between men in some village that belongs to the city. This is their opportunity and they
early learn to make the most of it. The mayor has
great power. He is judge, sheriff, tax collector, etc.
He has things his own way. When there is an

injustice done, there is no other local officers to
appeal to.

Prisons.

The prisons are cellars under ground, without
windows, damp and infested with flies. They are
seldom ventilated, and there is no bed nor other
furniture in them. The Government does not feed
the inmates. The friends of the imprisoned ones
bring bread and throw to them, and some of this even,
is sometimes picked up by the jailer and kept for his
own nourishment. No men are allowed to visit the
prisons, but wives or daughters are allowed to visit
their friends if they pay a fee to the jailer. The torture of the prisoners is regulated according to the
nature of their crime.

The common method of torture for thieves, robbers and murderers is to put the bare foot of the
criminal in a vise and squeeze it until he cries in
agony. If he gives the jailer some money or promises to give some the next time his friends visit him,
the pressure on the foot is lessened. If a man goes
to jail wearing good clothes, the jailer ofter changes
his own poorer clothes for the good ones.

Execution.

This is done in different ways. A prince from
the royal family has authority to behead men. Sometimes when a good friend of the king is appointed
governor, the king presents him with a knife. This

is a sign, and carries with it the authority, to behead
men.   Every prince, mayor or governor, who has
been given this authority, keeps two executioners.
The uniform of their office is a suit of red clothes.
These two men walk before the mayor when he goes
through the streets.   When the condemned man is
to be executed he is brought from the cell with hands
chained behind him, and with a chain about his neck.
He is surrounded by a group of soldiers with fixed
bayonets.   The guilty man has, perhaps, been in a
dungeon for several months; his clothes are in rags;
and having had no baths since first imprisoned, he is
very dirty; his hair and beard are very long and
shaggy.   A few steps before him walks the executioner, wearing a blood red garment and with a knife
in his hand.   Thus they proceed to the public square,
and before the assembled crowd the executioner
steps behind the kneeling victim, and, with a single
stroke of the keen knife, cuts his throat, and another
soul takes its flight, having completed its part in the
drama of life.   A common mayor who has not the
authority to behead, may kill criminals by fastening
them to the mouth of a cannon and sending a ball
through the body.

Another method is to bury the condemned alive
in a casket filled with cement leaving only the head
exposed.   The cement soon hardens and the victim
dies.   Sometimes when their crime is not very bad
the punishment is the severing of one hand from the
body.   If the man thus punished should commit

another crime, the remaining hand would be cut off.

If a Mohammedan becomes drunk with wine and gets loud and abusive, he is arrested, and the executioner punctures the partition skin between the nostrils of the drunken man, and a cord several feet long is passed through the opening. Then the executioner starts down the streets leading his victim. The man soon gets sober and is very much ashamed. Shop-keepers give the executioner pennies as he passes along the street.

Men who quarrel and fight are punished by tying their feet to a post, with the bare soles upward, and then whipping the feet until the flesh is bruised and bleeding and frequently the nails torn from the toes. The victims frequently become insensible under this punishment.

One good thing in the laws of punishment is that a Christian or a Jew is never beheaded. The Mohammedans consider the Christians and Jews as being unclean and think it would be a mean thing to behead them.

Princes, lords and counts are never beheaded. The most severe punishment for a prince is to pluck out his eyes. The method of execution for counts and lords is of two kinds. The king will send a bottle of sherbet to the condemned man which is given him in the form of a sweet drink, but it contains a deadly poison. He is compelled to drink this and soon dies. Another form is for the condemned man to be met by a servant from the governor after having taken a bath, and the servant cuts blood vessels in the arm of the condemned until death results from the loss of blood.

Thus it will be seen that the contrast in modes of punishment in a Christian nation and a Mohammedan nation is very great. The kind of punishment inflicted on criminals in any country grows out of the prevailing religious belief of that country. A religion that has much cruelty in it will lead a people to torture their criminals. But a nation whose religion is based upon love will deal with its criminals effectively, but as kindly as possible.

The writer has visited prisoners in both Persia and America and finds that the contrast of the prisons of the two countries, is like the contrast between a palace and a cellar. Prisoners in America ought to be very thankful for the humane treatment they receive under this Christian government.

LORDS.

The lords live in luxury. Their titles were not obtained by great service to the nation, or by high education. It descends from ancestors, and many ignorant and unworthy men bear this title. Wealthy merchants sometimes purchase the title for their sons. The titled class in Persia is very numerous. In one city of 30,000 inhabitants, there are more than five hundred lords. They own almost all the land in Persia. In some instances one lord owns as much as one hundred villages. All inhabitants of a village are subjects of the lord, and they pay taxes to him and also to the king. The men pay a poll tax of one dollar a year; a tax is levied on all horses, cows, sheep and chickens. The lord gets two-thirds of all grain raised by the farmers, and he expects a portion of all fruit raised, which portion is called a present.

All the lord's work is done by subjects without pay. When he builds a palace or cultivates a vineyard, he calls upon his subjects to do the work. He punishes his subjects if they rebel, and oftimes the punishment is so severe that death is the result. When a subject goes before his lord, he finds him seated in his private room before a window. The subject bows before approaching the window. When the lord is ready to listen, the subject comes to the window. He usually meets with a frown, and gets replies to his questions in a gruff voice. As a class, the lords are not strong physically; they eat and drink too much for their own good.

SCHOOLS.

There is no system of public or State schools in Persia. There are schools in all large towns and cities, taught by the priest in a room of the mosque. The schools are voluntary, no person being obliged to send his children. The students pay the priest each from five to twenty-five cents per month. Those who cannot pay anything, are admitted free. The priest's food is brought to him by the students. The ages of the pupils range from ten to twenty years.

These schools are for boys only. There are no schools for girls. If a girl gets any education at all, it must be from a private tutor. In the schools the text-books and history and poetry are in the Persian language; the Koran and grammar are taught in the Arabic language. Mathematics, geography, the sciences, and the history of other nations are never taught. When the pupils study, they read back and forth, and repeat words loud enough to be heard a block away. They imagine this is an aid to memory. The teacher has the authority to punish the students very severely. Sometimes the parent will take a child to the teacher, and will deliver him into the gentle keeping of the professor with the remark: "His bones are mine, but his flesh is yours; teach him, but punish him as you see fit." A post is planted in the school-room, to which a wild boy's feet are fastened, with soles upward, and the bottoms are whipped with heavy switches. This punishment is only for the worst boys. The religious teaching consists of quotations from Koran, and traditions about their prophets. The boys are very bad about fighting. The teacher does not protect the weaker, but urges him to return the blows he has received.

The students of one mosque often attack the students of a neighboring mosque, as they regard them as enemies. The most prominent university of the Shute Mohammedans, is in the shrine place of Karballa. All those who are to become Mujtahids, study at this place. In several of the larger cities they have schools of a higher rank than the ordinary mosque schools, in which a course of Persian literature is given. It is a pleasure to state that the late Shah, after his visit to some of the universities of Europe, founded a college in the capital city, which is called the Place of Science. The French, Russian, and English languages are taught, and the study of some of the modern sciences is being introduced. The college is only for princes and the children of rich people. The problem of Mohammedanism is to keep the common people ignorant so the priests can continue to rule them. Therefore the priesthood does not favor higher education. Some lords send their sons to Paris to be educated, but the ordinary young men have no opportunity for education.

CHAPTER II.

MOHAMMEDANISM.

In this chapter we wish to give a brief history of the religion of Islam, which has pressed its galling yoke upon the necks of this people of ancient Bible history until to-day they believe its tenets, and look for their reward from its flattering but deceitful promises.

Mahomet (or Mohammed) means, "Praise One." Some of the adherents of Islam (Mohammedanism) claim that Mahomet was the Holy Spirit which Jesus Christ promised to send into the world. Some also have advanced the belief that John the Baptist was Christ, and that the one to whom He referred when He said, "There is one that cometh after me," was Mahomet. Thus, you see, their conjectures and superstitions about this, their mighty defender, have entered into the sacred pages of Holy Writ, and wish to take from its Spirit-breathed tenets the truths which have nourished and fostered our Christian faith.

This great prophet of the desert, who converted wild Arabs to his religious scheme, was born 570 A. D., at Mecca. He was the only child of Abdullah and Halima, both from the noble family of Karush, who claimed to be the descendants of Ishmael and the hereditary guardians of the sacred Koolah mosque; in which is kept the holy stone which is worshipped by all Arabs.

The Mohammedans have many legends and traditions regarding the birth of Mahomet. They believed that the sun, from its place in the heaven, shone with a more brilliant lustre, attended with the seven colors of the rainbow.

The angels bowed themselves in honor to him, and sang a new song of victory. The trees were shaken as by a mighty wind, for this wonderful birth was not to be without manifestations. A seal of prophecy was written on his back in letters of light. Immediately after birth, prostrating himself upon the ground, he raised his hand and prayed. In answer, three persons, arrayed in garments as brilliant as the lustre of the sun, appeared in company with the angel Gabriel. One of the angels bore a silver goblet, another an emerald tray, and the third a silken towel. The angel Gabriel cut open the child's abdomen. The first personage poured in the water to wash away all sin, the second held the emerald tray beneath, the third dried him with the silken towel: and he was saluted by all, who denominated him "the Prince and Saviour of mankind."

His father died at the age of twenty-five, a short time before the birth of his son. He left to his widow five camels, a few goats, and a slave-girl, whose name was Amuia. At the age of six years, Mahomet had a fit of epilepsy. He frequently fell down, and foamed at the mouth, and snored like a camel. About this time his mother died, and he was reared by his grandfather, Abdulmutalib, and his uncle, Abutalif. For a little time he herded goats, a disreputable occupation among the Arabs, but he afterwards gloried in it, pointing to the example of Moses and David, saying that God never called a prophet who had not before been a shepherd. In appearance, he was of medium size, slender, but broad-shouldered, with strong muscles, black eyes and hair, an oval shaped face, a long nose, and a patriarchal beard. His step was quick and firm. He wore common garments of white cotton stuff. He was an adept at the art of patching, and mended his own clothes. He also assisted his wives in their household affairs. He had fourteen wives, besides concubines. He possessed a vivid imagination, also a genius for poetry and religious doctrine, but was not learned, and perhaps could neither read nor write.

He became servant for a wealthy widow named Khadijah, and made several caravan journeys in her behalf to Syria and Palestine, with great success. He afterward won the heart of the widow, and married her against the will of her father. The marriage was a happy one, and four daughters and two sons were born of this union. All of them died, except one little daughter, Fatima. Mahomet adopted Ali, his nephew, and gave his daughter Fatima in marriage to him. She became the mother of all the prophet's descendants. Mahomet loved his first wife fervently. After her death he cherished her memory as sacred, because she was the first to believe in his doctrines.

During his journey to Syria and Palestine, he became acquainted with the Jews, and obtained an imperfect account of their religion and traditions. At that time, the Jews had scattered their ideas among the Arabs who were tired of worshipping idols, and they immediately and with much earnestness, embraced the faith of one God. One of the men who were so turned, and who espoused this new idea of religion was Mahomet.

He became zealous to establish a religion throughout Arabia, which would compel men and women to worship one God, and to recognize him as His only prophet. He spent many days and nights in the caves of Mt. Hira near Mecca, in meditation and prayer in his zealous efforts to establish his faith. He began his preaching to the ignorant class of Arabs, teaching them that there is only one living God who created heaven and earth and all mankind. In the year 610 A. D., he claimed to have received a call from the angel Gabriel, while in a trance on Mt. Hira, who directed him to repeat many times the phrase "In the name of God." After this meeting, many times he communicated with Gabriel in these mountain caves, and saw many visions. At one time when almost discouraged, he waited for enlightenment in a vision for the authority to perform the duties of his office as a prophet; as the enlightenment was slow in coming, he intended suicide: but Gabriel, suddenly appearing, announced the words: "I am Gabriel, and thou art Mahomet, the prophet of God. Fear not."

After this assurance, he commenced his career as a prophet and founder of a new religion. His doctrines were gathered from three religions, the Jewish, Christian, and Arabic. He taught that there is only one God, Allah, Almighty God, ever present and working. Henceforth the revelation came to him from time to time, sometimes as the sound of a bell talking to him, at other times shining Gabriel made them. For the first three years he worked among his own family. Kadyah was his first convert. Omar, an energetic young man, his daughter, Fatima, his son-in-law Ali, and other faithful followers to the number of forty, were the first disciples of the new religion. These were very influential in spreading the new religion. He publicly announced that he had a command from God, and had been given the divine office as a prophet; and, as his notoriety spread, pilgrims flocked to Mecca and he preached to them, attacking the idolatry of the Arabians. In 622 A. D., he was forced to flee for his life from Mecca to Medina, a distance of 300 miles. This is what is called the famous Hegira, meaning the flight, (July 15, 622) from which the era of Isaen began. He was accepted as a prophet in Medina, and he preached that all infidels must accept one God and Mahomet as his prophet. His orders were, if men refused to believe the edict, "Kill them, plunder their property, and their wives and their daughters are for you." Ten years after the Hegira, with 65,000 Moslems, he made his last journey to Mecca, and subdued all Arabia upon returning to Medina. He died at his home, and in the arms of his favorite wife, Ayesha, June 8, 632, at the age of sixty-three years.

When on his death-bed and suffering from extreme pain and anguish, his friends expressed surprise that a great prophet should suffer so. He called their attention to the fact that one prophet of olden times was eaten by worms, while another was so poor as to have only a rag to cover his shame. He also stated that a prophet is not rewarded here, but hereafter. His last words were a prayer for the destruction of all Jews and Christians, because they were so hard to convert. He prayed, "Oh, Lord, let not my tomb be an object of worship; let there remain only one faith, that of the Islam, in all Arabia. Gabriel, come near me. Lord, pardon me. Grant me one joy—accept me into thy companionship on high."

Mahomet did not claim the power of performing miracles, but, since his death, some of his followers have attributed miracles to him; such as, when walking the streets, trees and stones would bow to him. It is said that he caused a flood of water to open up from the dry land. He also rode his horse, Barak, through the air, from Medina to Mecca. Not only this, but he went to the third heaven on the same horse. The only miracle Mahomet himself claimed was the revelation of the Koran. According to some Mohammedans, he had a good character. This, no doubt, is true in respect to his early life, but in later years he became degenerate, like the great Bible character, Solomon. He preached vanity. He never repented. He was full of passion. The doctrine of polygamy which he taught was the result of his own sensuality. One of his wives said: "The prophet loves three things: Women, perfume, and food."

The mighty means which served as the propaganda of the Islam religion was the sword. One of the teachings of this spreading viper, was, that one drop of blood shed for Allah, availed more than all prayers, fastings, and sacrifices. Everyone who should fall in battle, would be received in heaven as a martyr. His great command to the armies was, "Before you is heaven, behind you is hell." Inspired by this belief, the wild and superstitious Arabs pushed forward and subdued Syria, Egypt, and Palestine.

The Doctrines of Mohammedanism.

The Koran is to the Mohammedan what the Bible is to the Christian. It contains their creed and code of law. It was believed that the Koran was engraved on Mahomet's heart, and was communicated by him to the Arabs. His heart was the Sinai where he received the revelation, and the tables of stone were the hearts of believers.

The Koran contains one hundred and fourteen chapters and 6,225 verses. Each chapter begins with the formula, "Bismoolah alrahman alrahim;" "In the name of God, the merciful and compassionate."

The fundamental doctrine of Islamism, and the only one which is absolutely necessary to believe in order to be considered a Mohammedan, is, that there is but one God, and Mahomet is his prophet. The idea of God that is held by the Mohammedans, does not differ essentially from the Christian idea, except that they reject entirely the Trinity, and the holy sacrifice of Christ. They believe that a great number of prophets have been divinely commissioned at various times, among whom six were sent to proclaim new laws and dispensations. These six are as follows: Adam, Noah, Abraham, Moses, Jesus, and Mahomet. To the prophets were revealed certain Scriptures inspired by God. All of these have perished except three: The Pentateuch, the Gospel, and the Koran. The first two, they maintain, have been falsified and mutilated, because the Koran supercedes as to divine right, since Mahomet was the last prophet, and the Koran the final book of revelation.

The Mohammedans regard Christ with a reverence second to that of Mahomet. Blasphemy of His name is punishable with death. They deny that he is God, or the Son of God, though they consider his birth as miraculous. They deny the passion of our blessed Christ under Pontius Pilate, and assert that some other person suffered in his stead. while he was taken up to God. They believe that he will come again to destroy Anti-Christ, and his coming will be one of the signs of the approach of the final judgment.

The Moslems believe in the existence of angels with pure and subtile bodies, created of fire, who have no distinction of sex; neither eating nor drinking, but employed in adoring and praising God, interceding for mankind, keeping a record of human actions, and performing various services. Four of these personages are held in especial favor by God; Gabriel, who is employed in recording the decrees of God, and who revealed the Koran to Mahomet at different intervals; Michael, who is the special guardian of the Jews; Azrael, "the angel of death," who separates the souls of men from their bodies; and Israfe, who will sound the trumpet at the resurrection. There is a lower class of beings than the angels, also made of fire, but of a coarser nature, called Genii, who eat and drink, and are subject to death. Some of these are good, and some are evil. The chief of the Genii is Eblis, or "Despair," who was once an angel named Azazel, and who, having refused to pay homage to Adam, was rejected by God, and wanders over the earth until the resurrection.

Among the Moslems many opinions prevail. There are different views, especially in regard to the judgment, but the essential point agreed upon by all is, that men shall have rewarded to them that condition of happiness or misery, to which God shall judge them entitled by their conduct and belief during life.

The time of the resurrection is known only to God. Its approach will be indicated by certain signs, among which will be the decay of faith among

men, wars, seditions, tumults, an eclipse, the rising
of the sun in the west, and numerous other portent-
ous signs. After the judgment all must pass over
the bridge of the hair; the good will pass over easily
and speedily, the wicked will fall headlong into hell.

The delights of the Moslem heaven are for the
most part sensual, made up of pleasures especially
suited to each of the senses, while the torments of
hell consist chiefly of the extremes of heat and cold.
The Moslems hold that all who believe in the unity
of God will finally be released from punishment, and
enter Paradise. Those who deny the absolute unity
of God, idolaters and hypocrites, will suffer eternally
in hell. They believe in the absolute fore-knowledge
and predestination of all things by God, and sometimes in the responsibility of man for his conduct
and belief. Their practical religion, which they call
Din (religion), chiefly insists upon four things:
first, purification and prayer, which they regard as
together making one rite; second, alms-giving; third,
fasting; fourth, the pilgrimage to Mecca. Prayer
must be preceded by ablution. Cleanliness is regarded as a religious duty without which prayer
would be ineffectual. The Moslem prays five times
each day: soon after sunset, at nightfall, at day-break,
near noon, and in the afternoon at four p. m. The
times of prayer are announced by the Muezzins from
the towers of the mosques. In praying the believer
must turn his face toward Mecca. The wall of the
mosque nearest that city is marked by a niche.

Twice during the night the Muezzins call to prayer for those who wish to pray. Prayer may be said in any clean place, but on Friday they must go to the mosques. Women are not forbidden to enter the mosques, but they never do so when the men are at their devotions. Before prayer all costly and sumptuous apparel must be laid aside. Alms-giving was formerly of two kinds: legal, called Zekat, and voluntary, called Sedaka. At the end of the fast of Ramazan, every Moslem is expected to give alms, if he is able, for himself and each member of his family, a measure of wheat, or rice, or other provisions. The Moslems also lay great stress upon fasting. During the whole of the month of Ramazan, they fast from the rising to the setting of the sun. They neither eat nor drink, nor indulge in any other physical gratification. They observe this fast with great rigor. There are other days during which the fast is regarded as especially meritorious, though not obligatory, and fasting at any time is regarded as peculiarly acceptable to God. The Pilgrimage to Mecca, called Hadje, is a relic of the old idolatrous religion which Mahomet desired to do away, but which was too deeply rooted in the habits and interests of the people to be abolished. Hence he sanctified it and made it obligatory, having first destroyed the idols in the temple, and introduced new regulation. All Moslems, men and women, should, at least once in their lives, provided they are able, make the pilgrimage to Mecca. He who has performed this pilgrimage is entitled to prefix to his name the word "Hadje."

The Moslems regard the Koran not only as the rule of their religious, but also of their civil and social life. The following things are forbidden in the Koran: Eating of blood, or the flesh of swine, or of any animal that dies of itself, or has been killed by accident or by another beast, or has been slain as a sacrifice to an idol; playing of games of chance, whether with or without a wager; the drinking of wine or any other intoxicating liquor; the taking of interest upon money lent, opium, tobacco, coffee, etc. Murder is regarded by the Koran as a crime against individuals rather than against society. At the present time, murder in Persia is punished with death or a very great fine.

The ethics of the Mohammedan religion are of the highest order. Pride, avarice, revengefulness, prodigality, and debauchery are condemned in the Koran; while trust in God and submission to his will, patience, modesty, benevolence, liberality, love of peace, sincerity, truthfulness, etc., all those qualities that the Christian idealizes, are insisted upon everywhere.

Promise of Paradise.

The whole earth will be as one loaf of bread, which God shall hand to them like a cake. For meat they will have the ox, Balam, and fish. Every believer will have eighty thousand servants and seventy-two girls of paradise besides his former wives, if he should wish for them, and a large tent of pearls, jacinths, and emeralds. Three hundred fishes of gold will be set before each guest at once, and the last morsel will be as gratifying as the first. Wine will be admitted, and will flow copiously, without inebriating. The righteous will be clothed in the most precious silks and gold, and will be crowned with crowns of the most resplendent pearls and jewels. If they desire children, they shall beget them, and see them grow up within an hour. Besides the ravishing songs of the angel, Israfi, and the daughters of Paradise, the very trees will, by the rustling of their boughs, the clanging of bells suspended from them, and the clashing of their fruits, which are pearls and emeralds, make sweetest music. (From the Koran).

Prayer.

Prayer is the way by which a Mohammedan thinks he will go to heaven. There is no salvation by grace or atonement. Allah forgives his sins only through good works. Hence it is obligatory with every one to pray. Prayer is not a duty, but it is from love to God, or Allah, and is a yoke which binds him against his will. The Moslem always washes before prayer. While he is washing his hands, and his forehead, and his toes, he will say these words: "*Bism Allah rahman rahim;*" meaning, "In the name of the merciful God I am doing this holy service." He rubs his arms from the wrist to the elbow with

the tips of his fingers. He will wet his forehead, the
inside of his ears, and his toes. The worshippers
must have a seal from Mecca, which is made of clay,
and is about the size of a dollar. On it are the
words: "There is no God but God." He puts his
seal on the ground, stands straight up, and raises
both hands to his head, kneels to the ground, puts
his brow on the seal, then kisses it. Rising to his
feet, he puts his forefingers in his ears, and makes
numerous other gestures. As has been mentioned,
there are five seasons of prayer. The general place
for prayer is the mosque. Some pray on the street
and in open squares in the meadows, where they will
be seen by more men, and will be praised by the people. When I see them pray that way, it reminds me
of the words of the Lord about Pharisees on the
street corners. In the midst of his prayer, he will
stop and say a few words to the surrounding people
as a religious custom, or to censure children whose
noise at play may have interrupted him. The prayer
that is offered by a faithful Moslem is a selfish prayer,
and is entirely against the spirit and teaching of our
Lord. It reads, "O, Allah, I seek refuge to Thee
from Satan and all evil spirits. O Lord of all creatures, destroy all heathen and infidels and those who
believe in the Trinity, the enemy of our religion.
O Allah, make their children orphans, their wives
widows, and defile their abodes. Give their families,
their households, their women, their children, their
relatives, their possessions, their race, their wealth,

their lands, and their daughters as a booty to the Moslems, Thy only people, O Lord of all creatures !" I thank God for the religion of Jesus Christ, which teaches, "Love your enemies, bless them that curse you, do good to them that hate you," etc. Their religion does not require women to pray, but women pray sometimes.

There are three steps before every Mohammedan by which to go to heaven: prayer, fasting, and alms. As I have said above, Moslems have one month of fasting each year, which is called Ramazan. Their month begins with the new moon. They will fast from one hour before sunrise, until one hour after sunset. During this time they abstain from everything. The poor class work till noon. The rich do not work at all during this month. The day is spent in reading the Koran. Sick men are not compelled to fast during this month, but they will fast thirty days after recovering. They do not allow a Christian to speak to them. They think fasting and giving of alms will absolutely secure forgiveness of their sins, and entrance into heaven.

Jodie. (Magic.)

Magic plays a great part in Persia. Moslems and Christians, Armenians and Jews implicitly believe in the power possessed by evil-minded persons, of casting spells upon their enemies with a view to producing some baneful influence. Most of the spells cast upon persons are aimed at life, beauty, wealth, and the affections. They are much dreaded and the events connected with this subject that daily occur, are often of a fatal character. A Persian lady, however high her position, invariably attributes to the influence of magic the neglect of her husband, or the bestowal of his favor upon other wives; and the Persians and all other people of that country have a strong belief in the evil eye. It is supposed to be cast by some envious or malicious person; and sickness, death, loss of beauty, affection, and wealth are ascribed to it. When a child is found ailing from the supposed effects of the evil eye, it is considered a good test of the presence of the evil eye to place cloves on burning coals: as many of these cloves as explode show so many malicious persons to have left the effects of the Nezar (evil eye) behind them. Blue or gray eyes are more dreaded than dark ones, and red-haired persons are particularly suspected.

Dreams are greatly respected in eastern life. The young girl, early taught to believe in them, hopes to perceive in these transient visions a glimpse of the realities that are awaiting her; the married woman seeks in their shadowy illusions the promise of the continuation of the poetry of life, and firmly believes in the coming realities they are supposed to foreshadow; while the ambitious man strives to interpret them in favor of his hopes and prospects, often guiding his actions by some indistinct suggestion they convey to his mind.

FUNERAL CEREMONIES.

According to some verses taken from the Koran, earthly existence is but a fleeting shadow, seen for a moment, then lost sight of forever. Its joys and pleasures are all a delusion, and life itself is a mere stepping-stone to the celestial life awaiting the true believer.

"Know that this life is a sport, a pastime, a sham, a cause of vain-glory among you, and the multiplying of riches and children is like plants which spring up after rain, whose growth rejoices the husbandman; then they wither away and thou seest them all yellow: then they become stubble."

At the approach of death, no Imam, or servant of God is called in to soothe the departing spirit, or speed its flight by the administration of the sacrament. The friends and relatives, collected around the couch, weep in silence. If the departing one is able to speak, he will say, "Hallal Aelah," "forgiveness is requested and given." Prayers are repeated by the pious to keep away evil spirits that are supposed to collect in great force at such moments. Charitable donations or other acts of generosity are performed at death-beds; and frequently, at such times slaves are set free by their owners, for it is written:

"They who give alms by night and by day, in private and public, shall have their reward with their Lord. No fear shall come upon them, neither shall they grieve."

The moment the soul is believed to have quit the body, the women begin to utter wailings, some tear their hair, others beat their breasts in an outburst of genuine sorrow. Without loss of time, preparations are made for performing the last duties to the corpse, for the Persians can not keep their dead unburied any longer than is necessary for the completion of these preliminaries. If the death be that of a person of consequence, the Muezzin chants the special cry from the minaret (tower) and invitations are issued to friends and acquaintances for the funeral. Directly after death the eyelids are pressed down and the chin bandaged. The body is undressed and laid on a bed, "Sahat Yatib," (he is quietly sleeping), with hands stretched by the side, the feet put together, and head turned toward the Kilila (Mecca). A veil is then laid over the body. While the company is gathering and preparing for the prayer, the corpse, if it be that of a man, is taken into the court-yard on a stretcher and an Imam, with two subordinates, proceeds to wash it.

The formalities connected with this observance are of a strictly religious character, and consequently carried out to the letter. The first condition to be observed is to keep the lower part of the body covered, the next is to handle it with great gentleness and attention, lest those engaged in the performance of that duty draw upon them the curse of the dead. Seven small portions of cotton are rolled up in seven small pieces of calico. Each of these is successively passed between the limbs by the Imam while some hot water is poured over the bundles, which are then cast away one after the other. After the rest of the body has been washed, the formal religious ablution is administered to it. This consists in washing the hands and in wringing water into the hand three times, to the nose three times, three times to the lips, and three times from the crown of the head to the temples, from behind the ears to the neck; from the palm of the hand to the elbow, and then to the feet: first to the right and then to the left. This strange ceremony is performed twice. The Tahant (coffin) is then brought in and placed by the side of the stretcher. Before laying the body in the coffin, a piece of new calico, double its size, is brought. A strip about two inches in width is torn off the edge, and divided into three pieces, which are placed upon three long scarfs laid across the shawl. The calico, serving as a shroud, is next stretched in the coffin, and some of the cotton is used to stop the issues of the body, and is placed under the armpits and between the fingers and toes.

The body is then dressed in a sleeveless shirt, called "Kafan," and gently placed in the coffin. Rose-water is then sprinkled on the face, which is finally enveloped in the remainder of the cotton. The shroud is then drawn over and secured by the three strips of calico, one tied round the head, one around the waist, and the third round the feet, and the coffin is then closed down.

When all is ready, the guests are admitted; and the Imam, turning round, asks the crowd, "O congregation, what do you consider the life of this man to have been?" "Good," is the invariable response. "Then give Helat (forgiveness) to him." The coffin, covered with shawls, is then borne on the shoulders of four or more individuals who are constantly relieved by others, and the funeral procession, composed exclusively of men, headed by the Imam, winds its way in silence through the streets, until it arrives at the mosque where the funeral service is to be read. The coffin is deposited on a slab of marble, and a short service is performed by the congregation standing. This concluded, the procession resumes its way to the burial ground, where the coffin is placed by the side of the grave. A small clod of earth, left at one end of the excavation in the direction of the Kilila, takes the place of a pillow. The coffin is then uncovered and the body lifted out of it by the ends of the three scarfs previously placed under it, one supporting the head, another the middle of the body, and the third the feet, and lowered into its resting place. A short prayer is then recited, a plank or two laid a little distance above the body, and the grave is filled up.

At this stage, all the congregation withdraw, and the priest is left by the side of the grave, where he is supposed to enter into mysterious communication with the spirit of the departed, who is supposed to answer all the questions of his creed, which his priest puts to him. He is prompted, in the answer, by two spirits, one good and one evil, who are believed to take their places by his side. Should he have been an indifferent follower of the prophet, and forbidden to enter paradise, the evil spirit forces him to deny the only true God, and make a profession unto himself. A terrible battle is supposed to ensue in the darkness of the grave, between the good and evil spirits. The good spirit spares not his blows upon the corpse and the evil spirit, until the latter, beaten and disabled, abandons his prey, who, by Allah's mercy, is finally accepted within the fold of the true believers. This scene, however, is revealed to none by the priest, and remains a secret between Allah, the departed, and himself.

Part of the personal effects of the deceased are given to the poor, and charity distributed according to the means of the family. On the third day after the funeral, people will come from different parts of the country to comfort the family.

CHAPTER III.

MOSLEMS: MUHARRAN.

Cause.

When Mahomet was dying he announced, against his will, that his father-in-law, Abubekr, was his rightful successor. It was his real desire to be succeeded by Ali, his son-in-law; but he saw that Abubekr had a much wider influence than Ali, on the next generation. When Ali died there arose a division in the church. Hassan and Husan, the sons of Ali, claimed to be rightful Caliphs after the death of Abubekr. They claimed that their grandfather made Abubekr Caliph, because of his wide reputation and his old age, and therefore this office should not descend to his children. A great body of Moslems followed them, and at this time, the church divided into two parts, Shiah and Sunna. These sects became great enemies to each other, and war arose between them. Now Hassan and Husan, the two brothers, with many followers, began their campaigns, but Hassan was too timid to press his claims by battle. He met his death from a dose of poison administered by one of his enemies. The energetic young Husan continued to press his claims, but he had a very small army, composed of his relatives. Not long before this he was surrounded by the army of Yazed, one of the leaders of Sunna. He took

shelter beneath a large rock, and with his followers,
defended himself for three days and nights; but they
were finally driven to desperation by hunger and
thirst, and drawing their swords, they came out and
met the large army of men. After a brief contest
Husan and his men were overcome and Husan taken
prisoner. The killing of Husan and his followers
occurred in the month called Muharran. This entire
month, and ten days of the following month, are observed as a time of lamentation for Hassan and
Husan, and their followers, who were slain. During
this period every man and woman and child of the
Shiah, followers of Hassan and Husan, are under
obligations to wear black garments. The last ten
days of Muharran are observed in a fantastical spirit
as a revival of religion. This period is called Ashurah (ten days). The first seven days are for preparation. The mosques will be crowded with men and
women. The priest who is in charge of the services, goes to the mosque and stands on a high pulpit,
preaching to large crowds. His general theme is
tragic tales of martyrs and the manner of their death,
their last words, and the wailing and mourning of
their friends and relatives. Often during the con-
cluding words of a pathetic story, the entire audience, numbering thousands, will be deeply moved,
and slapping their foreheads with the palms of their
hands, will cry aloud. The mosques cannot accommodate all the worshippers during this period, so
some parts of the streets are laid with carpets and

rugs on which the people sit while listening to the preaching. The last three days are the most solemn. All the stores of the city are closed, and no business of any kind is transacted. At an early hour on these days the whole population except the old men and women, who stay at home to take care of the children, gather around the mosque. In and near the mosque, national and religious emblems are carried on a pole by strong men. These are very heavy and the stand-ard-bearers change every few minutes. They are followed by large crowds, sometimes numbering from 4,000 to 10,000 people. They march through the street, and each company goes from one mosque to another. Those who bear national emblems are fol-lowed by musicians playing mournful tunes upon such instruments as the drum, flute, etc., and hun-dreds of men marching with bare feet and bare breasts, shouting: "Hassan, Husan! Hassan, Hus-an!" and smiting upon their breasts with bare hands. There follows them another band with a Sayyid (a descendant of Ali), and all of them shouting, "Has-san, Husan!" and beating their breasts. Next comes a band of young men wearing, when the weather is warm, no garment except a pair of trousers. They hold in their hands a whip about fifteen inches long and one or two inches in diameter, made with small iron chains, with which they beat their bare shoulders and back, as they march shouting, "Yah, Hassan! Yah, Husan!" Then comes another band of Dervishes, bearing in one hand a knotty club, to

which is fastened nails, bits of brass, etc., and with
the other hand they beat their breasts and cry aloud,
"Yahu, Yamalhu!" which is the name of their gods.
These worshippers torture the flesh by beating it
thus. The marching commences early in the morning, and continues till 6 P. M. They continue in
this way until the ninth day. On the night of that
day is the time for old and prominent men to manifest their grief. They repair to the mosques with a
large supply of candles for illumination. A moolah
(priest) takes the head staff in his hand and in irregular procession they begin a lamentation which lasts
all night. While singing the words, "Shah Husan!"
they follow the moolah, who by his cry, "well-done!"
encourages them. Now and then he calls a halt, and
all beat their breasts with the cruel nigar. A man
sometimes passes around with a sponge or a piece of
cotton and wipes off their tears and presses them into a bottle, where they are kept as a remedy for
disease, and as a charm against evil influences. The
ancients buried these tear bottles in tombs as a proof
of their affection. Some Mohammedans, or Mussulmans, say that an angel collects these tears and keeps
them till the day of judgment as a witness of the
weeper's respect for the memory of Husan.

The greatest of all this occurs on Ashurah (tenth
day). At sunrise the same large crowds gather
around the mosque to start on the marches. On this
day there are also fresh recruits. In front of the
mosque is a band of one hundred or more men and

boys. They are bareheaded and uniformed with a white shirt over the other clothing, that reaches to the feet; they hold in the right hand a two-edged sword; the left hand rests on the belt of the soldier next in front. The leader standing at the head of the band recites their creed: "Alah is God, and the only God; Ali is his vicar." All the band repeats this creed. Immediately the leader smites his own brow with his sword, and the act is imitated by all his followers. Soon the faces and the white clothing of the men are red with blood. Bleeding in this way, they go marching through the street shouting, "Hassan, Husan!" and waving their swords in harmony with their step and voices. Their route can often be traced by drops of blood in the streets. When their zeal reaches a high pitch the blows are repeated on their brows. Fearing that zealous young men may lose all regard for life, and inflict upon themselves mortal blows, relatives and friends frequently walk near with long sticks in their hands to hinder them from such deeds.

This band first marches to the court house to be seen by the governor, for the freedom of some prisoner, and the request made then is always granted, no matter of what crime the prisoner is guilty. These bleeding men are considered as martyrs, and it is believed they would go to heaven if death should result from their wounds. After the parade is finished, the bloody shirts of these men are divided among their friends and kept as holy relics. The men who

compose these bands are usually the most wicked in
the city. They go through these ceremonies for the
remission of their sins, and to redeem themselves in
the eyes of others, but they usually continue in their
wickedness as before.

Another feature of the last day is a richly decorated hearse, containing a coffin in which lies a man
representing the corpse of Hassan. Beside the coffin sits a woman, representing the widow of Hassan,
dressed in sackcloth, and her head covered with mud.
Following the hearse are three Arabian horses, finely
saddled and harnessed. On two of them are seated
two girls, representing the two daughters of the martyr. The top of the girls' heads is covered with
mud and straw. The third horse is riderless, to re-
mind one of the missing martyr. Next following is
a large number of women, boys, and girls, and some
men, all with yokes about their necks and their
hands chained behind them, and mounted on camels.
These are to represent captives taken by Yazid, the
captain who killed Husan. Near them are men
with helmets to represent the soldiers of Yazid. They
are armed with whips, driving the women, men, and
children of Moslems into captivity. Next are seen
false heads raised on poles, representing the heads of
the enemies of Husan. Boys and men gather
around them, spitting and railing at them. All
sword-bearers, chain-strikers, and men beating their
breasts gather here. They make a great crowd and
a tremendous noise.

At 5 P. M. on the last day, the marching ceases
and the throng halts by some tents pitched in the
middle of the public square. The population of the
city is gathered around. Thousands of people are
gathered at windows and on house-tops near by.
Perhaps 25,000 or 35,000 people are present. The
sword and chain strikers approach the tents, and,
with a shout of victory, utter the names of Ali, Hassan, and Husan. They set fire to the tents and
burn them and their contents to the ground. They
imagine that their enemies are in the tents and are
destroyed by the flames; so it is a time of rejoicing.
The marching clubs disband and the active ones are
soon found at mosques drinking sherbet (a sweet
drink) as a sort of reward for performing their religious duty. It is not very safe for the Christian to
attend on these last days, unless with some honest
Mohammedan, for there is danger of his being killed
by some fanatical spirit of Moslem.

Heaven.

Mahomet declared in the Koran that there are
seven heavens. Above all is the heaven for prophets, martyrs, and those who die in battle for their
religion. In this heaven the greatest of all is Mahomet, the Mediator between God and believers.
The other heavens will be inhabited by believers.
Heaven is pictured as an earthly paradise, containing beautiful gardens, vineyards, and fountains of
pure water, and is capable of affording all kinds of

pleasure. The trees bear fruit continuously, some in blossom while others are bearing fruit, which is in abundance and growing on low trees so that a man can stand on the ground and pluck from the trees. Each vine bears 7,000 clusters of grapes and each grape contains 7,000 gallons of juice. The pastures are eternally green and in them grow thousands of varieties of flowers of different odors. There are no animals in heaven, as they are not needed. There are no dogs, cats, swine, nor unclean birds, as eagles and buzzards, etc.; but there are millions of birds whose melodies ring through heaven. The walls and gates of heaven are similar to those described in the 21st chapter of Revelations. Believers will spend eternity in the joys of a luxurious life in paradise. To an ordinary believer will be given seventy-two Houris, (or female angels). These creatures are described in the Koran as being fair, with rosy cheeks, black eyes, and in blooming youth, and their beauty the eyes of man have never seen on earth. Martyrs will have more than seventy-two Houris, the number increasing in proportion to the believer's merit. The believer will sit under a tree in a golden chair, or lie on a golden cot, while the birds sing their sweet songs and fairies will offer him choice, unfermented wine in a golden cup. Such is the Moslem's heaven.

These were the promises with which Mahomet aroused the enthusiasm of his followers. Fanatical zeal has been enkindled in men, and thousands have aided the spreading of this doctrine throughout the world. Saints will live nearer to Allah than ordinary believers, and will have conversation with him. No man can enter heaven unless he be a Moslem.

Hell.

As there are seven heavens according to degrees of integrity of believers, so there are seven hells. Johannam (hell) is beneath the lowest part of the earth. It is a great ocean of fire, without limit, and there are thousands of terrible flames and bad odors. Satan is there with all infidels, Christians, Jews, Fire-worshippers, and apostate Mohammedans. The torture of the latter will be worse than that of the others. There are in hell thousands of wild animals; as, lions, tigers, vipers, and serpents. Every lion has in his mouth 7,000 teeth and every tooth has 7,000 different stings or poisons. So with the tigers, and serpents. Every viper has 7,000 tails and on every tail 7,000 stings, and every sting contains 7,000 kinds of poison. The common drink of the inmates of hell is poison, drunk in iron cups. Their meals will be the flesh of animals and even their own flesh. Satan and his serpents will torture them with spears and swords of iron. There will be no rest for them day nor night. Men and women will gnash their teeth against their own children. All will be weeping and cursing and blaspheming. Hell is surrounded by walls of iron, over which none can escape.

Compare this religion with the religion of our

blessed Savior Jesus Christ, the only perfect God
and perfect man. He gave his life for the redemption of all the world, even of his enemies, that "whosoever believeth in him should not perish, but have
eternal life." Not only this, but he saves from all
sin, and keeps them saved from sin. Christianity is
as the sun shining in his fulness, while Mohammedanism is as the darkness of midnight. May God help
every one of his children not only to pray for this
people, but to help towards their salvation through
Jesus Christ, our coming King. May God help you
and me, dear reader, to give our lives for the salvation of the world.

It will be interesting to the reader to know something about the priesthood of Mohammedanism.
The Mujtahid, is the highest order of the priesthood,
but this order is divided into four degrees. The
members of the highest degree reside at Karhalali,
the secret city. It is believed by all Moslems that
the chief of this priesthood is the representative of
Mahomet. His position is the same as that of the
Pope of the Catholic Church, as he is believed to be
infallible. He rules over the entire clergy, and almost over the government. He has power to declare
holy war. When this chief dies there is great lamentation throughout the country, by those that have
confidence in him. The second degree of the Mujtahid, is called Arch Mujtahid. It is composed of
four priests, who reside in the four places that are
known as popular in Persia. One of these four

priests will succeed the high priest in Korbah, at his death. The third degree are common Mujtahid. Sometimes they are called Eulama (divines), on account of their way of living. They are executors of civil and religious law. No man can be a judge or lawyer unless he is a Mujtahid. These priests judge such cases as the division of property and charge a large fee. As a rule, he who pays the greatest fee, will win the case. Large fees are also made for writing legal documents in the transference of land and other valuable property. These men are usually very rich, and have from two to four wives. The fourth degree is called Mollak. They have business like Protestant preachers. Mohammedans have no preaching services as we have, except on holidays. The Mollak visits the sick and calls on families; teaches them to pray, and teaches some traditions to them. They also conduct funeral services; their meals are provided by students, who bring them some food each morning. The student who does this service gets twenty cents, the tuition fee for a month. He is highly respected in the community, and will receive large donations of wheat, grapes, etc.

Garments.

The Mujtahid wears long clothes of white linen. His long coat is made of woollen cloth, and his outer cloak is a robe which hangs to the feet. This coat is quite expensive, being made of the fur of animals, dyed yellow. He wears a girdle of white linen in many folds, and his turban is large and white. He wears shoes that cover half his feet. Men of all classes rise to salute him with their hands on their breasts. Many men kiss the shoes of the Mujtahid.

Sayyid.

Mohammedanism was divided into two great sects, Shiah and Sunna. Both hold Mahomet to be the prophet and savior of all human beings, and the Koran to be the Holy Scriptures, written by the finger of God, and given to Mahomet through the mediation of Gabriel. They differed in their belief as to who should be the true successors of the Prophet. Shiah claimed that Ali, son-in-law and nephew of the Prophet, was Caliph, while the Sunna claimed that four disciples of Mahomet were his true successors; viz., Abubekr, Omar, Sayyid, and Ohman. A discussion about their beliefs led them to war and bloodshed and gave rise to the two great divisions of Mohammedanism.

Persia belongs to Shiah, for she received Ali as her Caliph after Mahomet in high rank. These Sayyids are the descendents of the Prophets, and are very zealous to perpetuate their own sect. From the time of Ali, they have kept a careful record of their genealogy. This book is handed down from father to son, and serves as credentials to the Sayyidical tribe. Each family must have credentials at least two hundred years old. When these are worn by age and use, their leaders will draft copies and duly

certify them. Sayyid wears a dress different from
all others. He wears a green turban and girdle, so
that he is readily known whether alone or among the
people. The Sayyid turban is more precious to
them than the kingly crown, for it is the sign of
their glory. Their rank is higher than all other
degrees among men, and their high priest is honored
more than a prince. They are never smitten nor re-
viled, and if a Christian should lift his hand against
them that hand must be severed from the body. If
a Sayyid kills a man it is impossible to punish him.
The governor cannot punish him, for it would be sin
against God. It is believed that God created all men
for the sake of Mahomet and his descendants.

Dervishes.

Shiah Mohammedanism rests on two pillars, one
of which is the Dervishes. This is one of the most
holy orders of the Moslems. It corresponds to the
monasticism of Christianity. It contains several
degrees, such as asceticism, mendicantism, etc. It is
a voluntary consecration to Allah (God) and his
prophet, except in cases in which parents had dedicated their sons to the order. There are numerous
instances in which women without children made a
vow to Allah that if he would give them a son they
would consecrate him to God to be a Dervish. This
order contains members from all classes of people—
and men from the royal family. The Dervishes are
to tell the stories and traditions during the week days

in the streets. Friday is holy day among the Mohammedans. The Dervishes begin at 1 o'clock on that day to sing poems on the streets and continue until evening. Their poems are for the glory of Mahomet and Ali, for they believe these two men were the supreme creation of God. They are highly respected by all classes, from the royal family to the most humble, and if one should dare to beat or lay hands on one of them, it would be considered a great crime. The salutation is different from the common people. To the first "Yahoo," which means, "O living God," the response is,—"Yo malhoo," which means, "O God, giver of life!"

CHAPTER IV.

ALI ALLAH.

The author was reared by this people, and has labored among them, trying to bring them to a knowledge of the true Savior. They call themselves the Ali Allah (followers of God), and are frequently called Ali Allahi (believers of the Alli). Some have supposed that they were once Christians, but were conquered by the Arabs, and the name Ali substituted for Jesus, and that they afterwards forgot their origin. There is little proof of this supposition. There are at least seven sects of them in Persia.

The Ali Allah number more than one million souls. They reverence Mahomet more than any other prophet. He may be called their John the Baptist, the fore-runner of Ali. They call Ali the light of God manifested in the flesh, paying honor to him which is due to the Creator alone. Prayer, and sacrifices of fruits and animals, are offered to him. God is believed to have made frequent manifestations of himself to the Ali, and in his prophecy was the highest manifestation of the divine personality that appeared in the time of Abraham, Moses and David. Christ and Mahomet are therefore essentially the same person. They welcome Christians as elder brethren, many of them listening with pleasure to the gospel of the word of God. They have little regard for fasting, and alms-giving. The Mohammedan ritual of prayer teaches great veneration for shrines. They have certain prayers of their own, in Turkey, which are repeated many times a day. Light is a sacred emblem and symbol of the divine power. God is the central light from which the universe of spirit and life emanates, or is reflected, as a lamp in a room, whose walls are covered with many mirrors. Some of them hold to the pathetic conception, that not only prophets, but all angels, men, and the vital principle of animals and trees emanated from God and are of His essence. Associated with this idea is the doctrine of transmigration, and the final absorption of all in the bosom of the infinite, and the wicked are thought to enter into donkeys and other beasts of burden. Some of the Ali Allahs, however, hold to the Moslem doctrine of judgment and paradise; others deny the existence of Satan, and that evil is a principle in the heart of man. All men are regarded as sinners, but the prophets and pirs (elders) are sinless. Two of their rites come very near to the sacraments of the Old Testament.

Circumcision is made by the barber in the presence of the assembled relatives. The other rite greatly resembles the Passover; it is frequently celebrated at a certain time and place. Whoever wishes it at his house consecrates a lamb or sheep for the occasion. The victim is brought into the yard of the pir (elder) and is sacrificed to Ali by a man who has been formally appointed to this service. It is then cooked, blessed, and divided by the pir among

the men and eaten with great solemnity, and at the
same time a selection is read from one of their
sacred books. After the reading, raisins and nuts
which have been set aside as thank offerings for the
harvest, are distributed, and sherbet is drunk. This
sherbet is grape juice boiled down to the consistency
of molasses and mixed with water when desired for
drinking. Their story is that the sect originated
with forty persons, one of whom was Ali. God sent
them a grape from heaven and Ali pressed the juice
out of it, and the forty men drank it. From this
arose the custom of drinking sherbet. The sacred
book to which reference has just been made is in the
Turkish language, and is understood by the people
to be written by their divine incarnate Sultan,
Nahami, a pole of the universe, three or four centuries ago.

This sacred book is, for the most part poetic,
religious, autobiographical; and it holds a higher
place in their regard than the Koran. (Mohammedan
Bible.)

They have a service for the consecration of children. The father presents the child before his fifth
year, holding a nutmeg in his hand, in the presence
of the pir. After the ceremony it is divided and
given to the assembled company. The eldership
among the Ali Allahs is hereditary, or, at least, is
confined to the priests by family. Polygamy is rare,
but marriage is not restricted by laws of relation or
blood; they are much given to intermarrying. The

results are seen in the physical, and even in the social deterioration of the people.

PARSEE RELIGION (FIRE WORSHIP.)

This was the prevailing religion of Persia in ancient times. The general belief is that Zaradusht was the founder and reformer of this religion, as the religion and its followers are called by his name. Some think this religion and that of the Hindoo were originally the same, but were divided by some political affairs between the Ironians and the Aryans. The Hindoo branch took the Brahminian. The doctrine was changed somewhat after the separation, but the fundamental principles remain the same. Different opinions are given for the beginning of the Zaradusht religion. Some authorities date it as beginning at 500 B. C., before Christ, an opinion generally accepted.

Oroomiah, Persia, is claimed to be Zaradusht's native city, there being many good reasons for believing it to be his birth-place:

1st. His first followers were Persians and the religion was started in Persia.

2d. All Oriental scholars and writers suppose that this was his native city.

3d. In the district of Oroomiah I have seen several hills of ashes, one of them within a half mile of my home, covering about seven acres of land, and being one hundred and fifty feet high; all these hills were the places of worship of the fire-worshippers. Fire was their God, and a continuous flame was kept burning. On this hill are some fine old buildings which have been standing for hundreds of years, the works of some kings and notable persons of ancient times. Their book is called Avesta, which means "revelation." The language is called Zenda, from which the Persian language is derived. The founder of this religion taught as pure Monotheism as was taught by Mahomet. Zaradusht taught the existence of one diety, called Hurmized. He was giver of all good things as long as life existed, such as health, joy, happiness, etc.

The Vahu Mono (the good mind or realty), Akem Mono (or the naught mind or naught realty), Ahrommon, God of darkness, was the creator of all bad things, such as the devil, death, sorrow, hell, misfortune, etc. Zaradusht taught that there are two lives, one mental and the other physical. He believed in the immortality of the soul, and in two places for the departed; heaven, the place of the angels; and hell, the place of the devil and his followers. Between these two places there is a bridge of judgment over which only the followers of Zaradusht will be able to cross. They believe the son of Zaradusht will come before the general judgment in a spiritual form and will tell the time of the resurrection and judgment. The world at that time will be utterly steeped in the wretchedness and darkness of sin; then every thing will be renewed; death will be

slain; life will be everlasting. Holiness and righteousness will dwell in the new world. This Zoroas-
trian creed flourished until the time of Alexander
the Great, throughout the old world, and then declined. Again, under the Ardoshir, who claimed to
be the descendant of Zaradusht, the religion of his
ancestors was revived, and the lost parts of the holy
Avesta were found and put together; but unfortun-
ately was utterly destroyed in A. D. 640, by the followers of Mahomet. We now have in Persia about thirty
thousand Zoroastrians; they are called ungodly by
the Mohammedans. Most of them live in Karman,
on the soil of their motherland. They are very honest people and good citizens, especially kind to their
own brethren. They are intelligent, clean, handsome,
and faithful to their religion. The women have small
hands, small nose, clear complexion, with black eyes
and red cheeks, and are most beautiful. They do
not cover their faces in public except to Mohammedans, whom they consider wicked men. The women
are good, faithful house-wives, and honest to their
husbands.

A Parsee must be born on the ground floor
of the house of his parents as a sign of humility,
so that he may begin his life with good thoughts,
words and actions. The mother cannot go out for
forty days after the birth of her child; then she
washes herself with holy water made by the priest.
A Parsee rises early, washes his hands and face, then
offers his prayer towards the sun. They will not eat

anything that is cooked by one outside of the Parsee religion. Marriages can be contracted only with persons of their own creed. Polygamy is forbidden except after nine years of unfruitfulness. Then a man is allowed to marry another woman. Divorces are entirely forbidden. Persons guilty of the crime of fornication and adultery are *very* severely punished. In the case of a sick person, the priest will read some text out of the holy Avesta, as a consolation. After death the body is taken to the ground floor, the place of its birth, to be washed, anointed with perfumes, dressed in white and put on an iron grating. A dog is brought in to take a last look at the body. They believe it drives away all evil spirits. The relatives and friends go before, they bow down and raise their hands to their heads after touching the floor, as an indication of their last respects to the departed soul. Then the body is covered and two men carry it out of the house and give it to the pallbearers, who are dressed in white; they are followed by a great procession. The body is taken to the "Tower of Silence," where the last prayer is offered. It is then taken from the "Tower of Silence" and placed on an iron bier, and exposed to the fowls of the air, and to the sun, until the flesh is gone, and the bones fall into a pit beneath and are afterwards buried in a cave, or burned.

They believe that the holy fire was brought down from heaven. Only spirits can approach it, and even they must wear a half mask over their faces lest their

breath should defile it. It must never be touched by
the hands, but by instruments. Tobacco smoke is
prohibited, as the fumes defile the holy fire. They
say there are five kinds of fire, and great respect is
shown for them. They believe fire purifies all things.
A Parsee believes the soul of a dead man is walking
near the tomb for three days. The fourth day the
gates of heaven will be opened, and he will approach
the bridge of hair, where the good and evil deeds of
his life will be weighed in the balance of justice. If
the good deeds outweigh the bad, he will pass over
the bridge into heaven; if the bad are heavier, he
will fall beneath the bridge into hell. This is only
a brief history of these poor people without Christ
or hope of heaven.

BABEISM.

The Mohammedan religion is divided into several
different sects, something like other isms of the
world. This division greatly weakened it. The
Babe sect was started by Mirza Mahomet, Ali of
Shiroz, the city in which lies the most educated and
poetical scholars of Persia. He began to plan this
new religion at the age of eighteen, but did not re-
veal it until he was twenty-five. The foundation of
his faith was that Mahomet, like Christ, in his later
life taught that in the latter days there would be a
millennium. They have a tradition that when all
the prophets die, or are killed by their enemies, a son
six years old, by the direction of Allah (God), hid in

an unknown well, will remain there until the millennium. It is believed that he will rule over the Mohammedans in the last days. He is to lead his victorious armies, conquer all the world, and this will become the universal religion.

Mirza Mahomet Ali based his doctrine upon this theory, but changed it somewhat. At the age of twenty-five he made several pilgrimages to shrines, such as Mecca, Medina, etc. At first he began to teach this doctrine to his relatives and confidential friends until it was established in their hearts; then he began to preach to the public that he was Mehdeialzomon. He taught that every age must have its own prophets, inspired by God. He claimed that he was inspired and had frequent communications from God, telling him how to direct the people. He openly claimed to be Mehdeialzomon, and taught that the priesthood and religion were corrupt, and that he was appointed to reform them. He did not oppose the Koran, but said every age needed a new book. He claimed to have received a Bible from God. This book is called Bayan (exposition). He taught the equality of the sexes, and paid homage to women, and showed that it was against the law of God to marry more than one; and it was against society and the happiness of the woman to marry more than one man. Divorces which were common among Mohammedans, were not allowed by the new sect; the place of woman among them is the same as it is among the Christians. He taught that the spirit of charity ought to be like fire in the hearts of his followers. He said that we cannot please God, if we see our brothers in need and do not help them; when we pray he will not hear us, and if we worship, he will turn his face away. His followers are very kind to the people of other faiths. The converts are intelligent and well educated. This doctrine is spread all over Persia.

Among his followers were two important men: Malah Hussein and Hajee Mahomet Ali. He called them his right- and left-hand supporters. Another convert of importance was a lady who was highly educated, and traveled with two assistants from State to State, preaching the new doctrine. She never met Babe, the founder, and knew him only through letters. She said that God had endowed her with unusual gifts for this holy cause, and by her power and eloquence she made many converts.

Babe was a tall man with black hair and eyes and a long beard, patriarchal in his conversation with people. He made himself a servant to all people; was a great orator and deep thinker, and wrote many poems. The epistles to his disciples were philosophical, and the words in his sermons touched the hearts of his people. When the Mohammedans came, the doctrines of Babeism were spreading among the people. The priesthood and government severely persecuted the disciples of the new faith.

The disciples were scattered to different parts of the country which resulted in greatly spreading the new faith. At this time he appointed eighteen of his apostles as guards of the new faith, two of them being women, and he requested that this rule should be followed in the future. About this time Babe and his twelve disciples were arrested at Shiroz and taken to Isphahan and imprisoned. He was finally banished to Makoo, between Persia and Russia, and his doctrine soon prevailed there. At last the priesthood and government decided to bring him to Tahreez to be shot. Babe and his twelve disciples were hanged to a wall before the soldiers; before the order to fire, the disciples were given a chance to save their lives by denying the new faith. Only one denied and was saved, the others being willing to die. When the soldiers were commanded to fire all were killed except Babe; the ball striking the rope in his case, and letting him drop to the ground uninjured. He ran into a house and tried to escape, but was soon captured and killed, after being again promised freedom if he would only deny his faith. After the killing of Babe his disciples suffered great persecutions. This began at the reign of the Shah. Many fanatical Babeites tried to kill the king, so, fiery persecutions arose against them, and about twenty thousand were killed.

The torture was very cruel, and the heroic death of the Babeites affected many prominent men in the capitol, making them believe in their faith. After this great massacre, which occurred in A. D. 1850, the believers in Babe held their faith in secret.

Eighteen men who were not generally known, were
appointed guards of their faith, and a very learned
young man was appointed to take the place of Babe.
His title is Baha, and he resides in Akra, a small city
in Turkish Ter. Even to-day they are very earnest
in spreading their religion; but the work is done in
secret by the apostles going from place to place, being known by a secret sign.

The enmity between them and orthodox Mohammedans has been very severe from the time of the
killing of Babe until the present day. The Babeites
have made several attempts to kill the Shah. In
their first attempt they failed; but two years ago,
while the Shah was worshipping in the holy place of
the Mosques, he was shot by a Babeite, who had dis-
guised himself as a woman. Some thought that the
government would again persecute them; but it never
did, because of some hindrance which would not permit it. The Babeites are very good friends to Christians, and have great confidence in them. Sometimes they will lodge in the houses of Christians and
eat with them; this a strict Mohammedan will never
do. They really allow the Christians to preach to
them and discuss religious subjects; yet it is a hard
matter to convert them, for one must know their
manner of life and religious doctrine to meet their
arguments successfully. When the Christian shows
the superiority of Christ and his doctrine over that
of their Prophet Babe, they are forced to silence.

They are now making many converts from Mohammedanism; and it is believed that the time will come when religious toleration will be obtained by them. This will also give the Christian a great opportunity to preach Jesus Christ who saves from all sin, and gives satisfaction to the hungry soul. This is the purest and sweetest religion in the world. Reader, have you this religion that satisfies, fills and thrills the soul, and makes life worth living? If not, the author has it, through Jesus, and recommends it to all who want to enter heaven, and live forever with the blood-washed throng. Hallelujah! Amen.

CHAPTER V.

KURDS.

The Kurds are the wildest tribe of nomads in all Asia. They have been known in Europe as raiders for a long time; and during the last three years, they have attracted the attention of the civilized world by their horrible massacres of the Armenians. I hope it will be interesting to the reader to know something about the life of this tribe. In regard to their ancestry, it is very difficult to trace it back to the original stock from which they came, as they have lived under the authority of several governments. It is believed that in their blood is a mixture from the old Assyrians, Chaldeans, Babylonians, and Arabians. It is supposed that some of the wildest characters in all of the ancient nations formed the tribe of the Kurds, of which there are to-day about 1,000,000. Their dwelling place is in the Kurdistan Mountains—a large territory lying between Turkey and Persia, but most of it being in Turkey. The Kurds are generally subjects of these two countries, but are a band of outlaws beyond the control of any government. Those who live in the mountains pay no taxes to either Turkey or Persia; but those who reside in the villages of the plains are required to pay taxes as other citizens do. Great numbers of those dwelling in the mountains and deserts are nomads, traveling about with their flocks and herds. A Kurd is very wild and independent; he would rather live in a cave, or under a projecting rock and be free, than to live in a palace, and be subject to higher authority.

Occupation and Character.

Some of them are nomadic, not having any fixed habitation, but wandering in annual circuits. Spending their summers in the cool places of Northwestern Persia, and the winters in the milder parts of Assyria. It is interesting to watch them during these migrations, moving with families, tents, flocks, and herds, the hardy females bearing their little children in cradles on their backs. The older children are packed in large sacks, with only their heads sticking out. Often with lambs to balance the pack, they are slung across the back of a cow or an ox. In this way they move as the season advances; and midsummer finds them near the summit of the mountain, in the neighborhood of perpetual snow, among cool rills, rich pastures, and blooming flowers. Some Kurds are also agriculturists, living in the villages and tilling the soil on the plains and hillsides. It is quite amusing to watch them on their way to work, dragging their sluggish limbs; you would think they would drop to sleep at any moment. They will waste two hours before they begin work. After an hour of pretended labor, in which they have not really accomplished anything, they will sit and take a smoke. Then they rise again, with long sticks in their hands, with which they urge on the oxen which draw the

wooden plows, but scarcely have they resumed their
work before they are ready for another rest and another
smoke. Then down the hill the laborers (?) go for a
draught of cool water from the spring in the valley
below. In this way they carry on all their work.
Poor creatures, they are good for nothing. Others
are shepherds. It is really inspiring to see their devotion to their sheep;—to see the shepherd as he
goes before his flock, with staff in hand, on which
hangs a bag containing his food for the day. Now
and then he whistles. In this way he indicates to the
sheep that he wishes them to travel, which they do
immediately. He has also given them names, and
often calls his favorites to him and pets them. Sometimes you can see him sitting on a rock, with his fond
flock gathered around him, while he sings and plays
his flute. How beautifully this illustrates the words
of our Lord, "He calleth his own sheep by name,
and leadeth them out; and when he putteth forth his
own sheep, he goeth before them and the sheep follow him; for they know his voice." This is a beautiful picture of the Kurd. Let us look at him, however, as he rides his Arabian steed, with his gun upon
his shoulder, sword at his side, and spear in his hand.
He is now a veritable fiend of death, his dark eyes
filled with rage, and his sullen countenance fearful
to look upon. These warriors sleep most of the day,
but at night they start on their robbing expedition.
They ride down into the numerous villages in the
valley, and carry away the cattle and flocks. No one

dares molest them, as the very name strikes terror to the hearts of the people. Stealing is their occupation, as they believe God created them for this purpose only. I have traveled among them. Conversing with them, I have asked, "Why do you steal?" They will invariably say, "This is our occupation." The most of them are making their living in this way, and are always ready to defend their cause. Any one who has not killed two or three men, is not thought worthy to live. As a rule, Kurds are a very cruel people, and are well adapted to the regions which they occupy. Like Ishmael their hand is against everybody, and everybody's hand is against them. They are very brave people, having no fear whatever on the battle-field.

In the Turko-Russian war, they are said to have been Turkey's best soldiers. From the Persian Kurds, several regiments are raised for the Persian army, that always prove themselves the bravest soldiers on the battle-field. Kurds are very fond of fighting, and the slightest offence will make them an enemy, and they will at once seek revenge. They are very nimble in climbing the mountains, and in running and fighting. Kurds like to revile an enemy, and are continually trying to find some means for a quarrel, as it is their nature to quarrel and fight. Brothers often become angry over a small matter, go out, and kill one another. Kurds think no more of killing a person than we do of killing a chicken. They are a people having no fore-thought whatever,

having a saying among themselves, "God will be
merciful for the morrow." They are also very rash,
acting on the impulse of the moment, never thinking
of the consequences. They will never forget a kindness shown them. If a Kurd eats the bread that is
given him by anyone he will never rob the giver,
as this is against their laws. Travelers, coming to
their tents or caves, are treated very kindly. They
will offer a stranger food and drink; but it would not
be well for him to show them money while there, as
they would follow him. The most prominent characteristic of the race is thieving. Almost all thieves
in Persia and Turkey are Kurds.

Religion.

In religion the Kurds are Mohammedans of the
Turkish faith, having chiefs (priests) who are called
Sheiks, and are honored as a god. The people kneel
before a chief, and kiss his hands, clothes, and shoes,
and ask for his blessings. To penitent ones he will
promise that he will ask "God" to forgive their sins.
He has absolute control over all laymen. They believe that his words are inspired truths, and obey him
implicitly. One leader of this type made war with
Persia fourteen years ago. He had under his command 100,000 Kurds, whom he told not to be afraid
when they saw the big cannon of the Persians, prom-
ising them that, by the help of Allah, meaning God,
he had his hand over the mouth of the guns, and the

Persians could not hurt them. So, believing this statement, the poor ignorant Kurds rushed wildly into the face of the guns, and many thousands were slain. There are priests of different ranks, but all are subordinate to the Sheik.

Kurds, as a rule, are more superstitious and fanatical than the Mohammedans of Persia and Turkey. They have no written language, but speak a mixed language derived from Persians, Arabians, Syrians, etc. The Kurds have been called "wild asses of the desert," thirsty to shed blood, and eager to plunder. Among these people live many Nestorian and Armenian Christians. The Kurds treat the Christians very well, not because they love them, but because their services are profitable. If such had not been the case, the Kurds would have slaughtered them long ago. Any Kurd in a Christian village is considered rich; for he has the Christians' labor the year round. All they have belongs to him. If they have wives and daughters, he will take them, and they will work for him while he sits around. Women and children are treated unmercifully. The lives of the Christians are in the hand of those unmerciful people. The Christians try to teach them Christianity, hoping by this means they may make their yoke easier.

Kurdish Houses and Women.

The most of the summer they live in tents in the cool places on mountain slopes and valleys. Their winter houses are built underground, most of them having a single room, with one or two small holes on top for light. In the day-time they are all away; toward sunset they come in one by one, at least a score of them, men, women and children; but already the hens have found their resting place, sheep, oxen and horses, each in their corner. After it is quite dark, coarse, stale bread and sour milk are brought out for supper. Two spoons and one big dish are sufficient for all, and each in his turn tries the spoon. Of course this is always done in the dark, as they have no lights. Now it is bedtime, and one after another finds his place under the same quilt, without a pillow or bed, except some hay spread on the floor. In a few minutes all are fast asleep, and soon the heavy breathing and snoring of men and cattle are mingled. The effect is anything but harmonious. The temperature of the room is sometimes as high as one hundred degrees, Fahr.; and swarms of fleas (one of which would be enough to disturb the rest of an entire American family) attack the wild Kurd; but he stirs not until morning, the fleas being exhausted sooner than the men.

Their women wear an exceedingly picturesque costume. They have dark complexions, with eyes and hair intensely black. Their beauty is not of a refined type; but by a mass of paint is made sufficiently attractive for their easily-pleased husbands. Almost all the work, both in and out of doors, is done by the women. Early in the morning when they are through their home work, they hasten to the fields to attend the flocks, or gather fuel for use in winter. In the evening they come in with burdens on their backs, apparently heavy enough for two donkeys to carry. So industrious are they, that they frequently spin on the road to and from work, singing all the while, seeming as happy as if all the world were theirs. The difficulties and ailments of womanhood are nothing to them. A woman with child will go out among the rocks, climbing the mountain heights. Her time of labor is at hand, but she does not cease her usual toil. In the evening the woman may be seen coming singing down the mountain, a heavy burden of fuel on her back, and in her arms the child to which she has given birth that day. Even this the men do not appreciate or reward. They will not hesitate, when it is raining, to drag the women from the tent in order to make room for a favorite steed.

THE YEAZIDES.

One peculiar people who live in Persia are the Yeazides. They worship the devil. No one knows from what race this people came, as they say they are not the seed of Adam. Their name means, "seen," or "found." Their tradition is, that darkness at one time came over Adam, and this circumstance made him sad, and that Satan went to Adam and said, "Why are you sad?" Adam answered, "Because darkness has come upon me." And Satan then

said, "Give me some of your children, and I (Satan)
will bring light upon you." This Adam was unwil-
ling to do; and after he had hidden his children, Satan was so cunning that he found some of them, and
kept them for himself. He told them that he was
their father or creator, and they were his children.
They say he taught them a written language, which
is different from all others. They will not read it
before strangers, but entirely to themselves. These
people are very strict in their habits; they live in
Mossoul, Halab, Bagdad, and Mardin. There are
several different classes, which, from ancient times,
have constituted one tribe, separate from all other
people. They desire to be independent in their
government, and at present they have their own king,
but he rules over them only in religion. For this
they pay him a salary of one million dollars per year.
These people keep the holy days of Christians, such
as Christmas, Easter, the Ascension of Christ,
etc. Five hundred years ago they were a Christian
people; but they were turned from Christianity by
the sword of their enemies. O! how these people
need the gospel of Jesus Christ! May God help
some of his children to send it to these poor and
needy people.

Perhaps it will be interesting to some reader to
know something about a race of people that was
brought into Persia some years ago. Their dwelling
place is Suldooz. In their coming to occupy this
country it was made a province, with a government

separate from that of the Kurds, among whom they dwell. They are subject to no taxation from the general government, except an outfit of five hundred horsemen, in time of war. They are called by the Kurds, Karapapaks (black hats), referring to their black lamb-skin caps, which are the common covering for the head in Persia. Perhaps they are comparing them with their own imposing head-dress, which consists of huge turbans that are made of a very large shawl, striped, red, and white, coiled around a broadcloth cap, until the whole thing assumes the shape of a great shield. It is fastened to the back of the head in a nearly perpendicular position by a handkerchief or belt passing around the forehead. These turbans give their naturally wild, lofty air a very impressive appearance. These people are not destitute of interest to the missionary. Their private morals are less corrupt, and they are more tolerant toward nominal Christians. Both men and women are very handsome; and the striking Kurdish costume gives a great brilliancy and picturesqueness to this remarkable city. The short, sleeveless jackets of sheepskin, with black wool outside, which the men now wear over their striped satin vests, and the silver rings in the noses of the girls give them something of a "barbarian" look. And, indeed, their habits appear to be much the same as those of their Karduchi ancestors in the days of Xenophon, except that in the interval they have become Moslems and teetotalers.

Here they are Sunna, and consequently do not
clash with their neighbors, the Turks, who abhor the
Kurds of the mountains as Kizilbashes.

Their Kurdish physique is very fine. In fact, I
have never seen so handsome a people; and their
manly and highly picturesque costume heightens
the pleasing effect, intensified by their lithe, active
figures.

The cast of their features is delicate and somewhat sharp; the mouth is small and well formed; the
teeth are always fine and white; the face is oval; the
eyebrows curved and heavy; the eyelashes long; the
eyes deep-set and intelligent; the nose either straight
or decidedly aquiline, giving a hawk-like expression;
the chin slightly receding; the brow broad and clear;
the hands and feet remarkably small and slender.
The women, when young, are beautiful; but hard
work and early maturity lead to a premature loss of
form, and to a withered angularity of feature which
is far from pleasing, and which, as they do not veil,
is always manifest. The poorer Kurds wear woolen
socks of gay and elaborate patterns; cotton shoes like
the gheva of the Persians; camlet trousers, wide at
the bottom like those of sailors; woolen girdles of a
Kashmir shawl pattern; short jackets and felt jerk-
ins without sleeves. The turban usually worn is peculiar. Its foundation is a peaked felt cap, white or
black, with a loosely twisted rope of tightly twisted
silk, wool, or cotton wound around it. In the girdle
the khanjar is always seen. Over it the cartridge

belt is usually worn; or two cartridge belts are crossed over the chest and back. The girdle also carries the pipe and tobacco pouch, a long knife, a flint and steel, and sometimes a shot pouch and highly ornamental powder horn. The richer Kurds dress like the Syrians. The undergarment, which shows considerably at the chest and at the long and hanging sleeves, is of striped satin, either crimson and white, or a combination of brilliant colors, over which is worn a short jacket of cloth or silk; also with long sleeves, the whole richly embroidered in gold. Trousers of striped silk or satin, wide at the bottom; loose mediæval boots of carnation-red leather; a girdle fastened with knobbed clasps of silver as large as a breakfast cup, frequently incrusted with turquoise; red felt skull-caps around which they wind large striped silk shawls, red, blue, orange, on a white or black ground, with large, fringed ends hanging over the shoulders and floating in the wind as they gallop. In their girdles they carry richly jeweled khanjars and pistols, decorated with silver knobs, beside a number of other glittering appointments. The accoutrements of the horses are in keeping; and at marriages and other festivals the head-stalls, bridles, and breastplates are completely covered with pendant silver coins. The dress of the women is less splendid than that of the lords. It consists of a blue cotton shirt; very wide trousers, drawn in at the ankles; a silver saucer on the head, from which chains depend, with a coin at the end of each; a square mantle hanging down the back, clasped by two of its corners around the neck, and many strings of coins around the throat; a small handkerchief is knotted around the hair, and in presence of a strange man they hold one end of this over the mouth.

CHAPTER VI.

NESTORIANS.

I wish to say a little about the nation of the Nestorians, or Syrians. They are descended from Shem. Aram, the fifth son of Shem, was the father of the Aramites. The name means Syrian. They dwelt in Padan-aram (Gen. 31:8; 25:20). Chaldea was another name used for the same country. (Acts 7:5.) Another name for it is Bit Nahren, "between two rivers"—the Tigris and the Euphrates. In European languages the country is also called Mesopotamia. (Judges 3:8.)

But my object is to let you know something of this nation. And first I will speak of their language. Educated men of many countries think that this is the language which our first ancestors used to speak, even Adam and Eve in Paradise. "Adam," in the Syrian language, means "dust," and "Eve" means "life."

The new race which began to populate the earth after the great flood had as its originators the three sons of Noah—Shem, Ham, and Japheth. The descendants of each of these developed into a distinct race, with peculiar characteristics and separate places of abode. The descendants of Ham spread out over the steppes of Arabia, and to the Persian Gulf, and the territory of the Nile. The Egyptian race, as well as the Babylonian, is of Hamite origin. The descendants of Ham were and are still heathens.

The family of Japheth betook itself to Armenia and the northern region. They, too, lacked a true knowledge of God, and wandered in the darkness of heathenism.

The Semites (descendants of Shem) settled in the middle and southern district of the fruitful and, as regards climate, favorite Asiatic borderland. One place, for example, well known and famous as a habitation of many Semitic princes, is Elam, which derived its name from Shem's oldest son, who first took up his abode in that region.

Shem's second son was Assur (Asshur). He dwelt in the land which is now called Assyria after him. He built great Nineveh on the River Tigris, the rival of mighty Babylon.

Arphaxed, the third son of Shem that the Bible mentions, was the ancestor of the Chaldeans, and the fourth son is called Lud: from him descended the Lydians, in Asia Minor.

The fifth and last son of Shem was Aram (Gen. 10:22), from whom the Arameans have their origin. These (who in later times were also called Syrians) had their original dwelling place in the country which the Bible calls Padan-aram (Gen. 25:30; 31:18), and also "Ur of the Chaldees" (Gen. 11:18; Acts 7:4). A more comprehensive name of the same region was Bit Nahren—that is, "between two rivers," namely, between the Tigris and the Euphrates. Therefore in Judges 3:8, and also in Acts 7:4, the Greek name Mesopotamia is found, which means the same thing.

From this their native dwelling place, the descendants of Aram spread out westward from the Tigris (Dan. 10:4) and the Euphrates (Gen. 2:4) into the region later called Syria, whose capital was Damascus. They settled there in the time of the Israelitish kings, with whom they lived in continual feud, and fought many battles. (II Sam. 8:18; I Kings 11:24.) The Syrian kingdom was not a unity, as it embraced a number of smaller kingdoms, the greatest of which had Damascus for its capital.

The great Assyrian king made an end to this union of States, for he appeared in this region with a great army in the year 750 B. C., and having vanquished the Syrians, deported a great majority of them to Assyria. The same fate befell them again in the time of the Chaldean monarchy, for Nebuchadnezzar, their king, in a similar manner removed a large portion of the people, and colonized them in Babylon. At this time the Syrians are said to have acquired the name Chaldeans. After the destruction of the Chaldean monarchy, the Persians came to the rulership of Babylon; after them the Greeks (under Alexander the Great), and after the Greeks the Romans.

Concerning the origin of the Syrians, we learn the following:

According to one authority an old king of these people was called Syris, who built a great city which took the name Sur (Tyre) after him; and soon, in carrying on its important commerce, became so mighty and flourishing that it gave its name to the whole land (II Sam. 24:7.) It was built on an island in the sea. Alexander the Great had to besiege it for seven months before he could take it. According to others, the name Syrian comes from Asshur, which among Europeans is called Assyria.

As regards the Syriac language,—so assert the antiquarians who have traced it,—it is a very old language; perhaps the oldest in the world, because Adam and Eve spoke it, which can be shown from the Syrian form of their names. This language was spoken in all Assyria, Chaldea, and Syria, at the time mentioned above; it was, in its basis, the same language, with only a few dialectic variations. Besides the Syriac they still knew in these regions Hebrew and Arabic, both being branches of the same original language to which the Syrian belongs. Each of these three languages claims to be the oldest, especially the Hebrew, with the argument that the *Torah*, (Old Testament) was written in Hebrew; and they claim that Adam and Eve spoke Hebrew. But this argument can by no means prove the point claimed; for it admits of the objection that Moses composed the *Torah*, and we naturally suppose that he composed it in the language which was familiar to him, that is, the Hebrew; for he was a Hebrew. Others still hold the Sanskrit, which was spoken in India, to be the oldest, because they find in it many parts of other languages.

Fragments of the Syriac and Aramean languages

are found scattered here and there in the Bible. In Gen. 31:47, Laban, of Aramea (or Padan-aram, or Bit Nahren, or Mesopotamia), calls the heaps of stones *Jegar-sahadutha*; Jacob calls it *Galeed*—that is "witness."

Jegar-sahadutha was a place in Padan-aram, in the same language as that spoken in Padan-aram, and also in Ur of Chaldea. And it was from there that the patriarch Abraham moved toward Canaan.

A better documentary evidence is II Kings 18:26. Rabshakeh, a powerful leader in the Assyrian kingdom, spoke Hebrew with the Israelites who stood upon the walls of Jerusalem. But the officers of Hezekiah, the Jewish king, asked him to speak in Aramean, in order that the native people might not understand and become afraid. From this it follows that the officers of Hezekiah at that time all understood Aramean, inasmuch as the Aramean kingdom was extensive and considerable.

After the Jews had staid seventy years in exile in Babylon, the Chaldean language had become familiar to them, an example of which is to be found in Daniel 2:9; and there are a few portions of Ezra and Nehemiah that were composed in the Chaldean or Aramean language. Also the edict of Cyrus, which permitted the Jews to return home and rebuild their city, although it is addressed to the officers and governors west of the Euphrates, is proclaimed in the Chaldean language. (Ezra 1:1.)

In the time of Jesus Christ this language was in

very general use, for it had been brought back by the Jews returning from Babylon. Christ himself very often spoke it. One can take as evidence of this Matt. 27:46, "Eli, Eli, lama sabachthani?" that is, "My God, my God, why hast thou forsaken me?" Also Mark 5:41, "Talitha cumi;" that is, "Maid, arise." Mark 7:34, "Ephphatha;" that is, "Be opened." Rom. 8:15, "Abba Baban;" that is, "Dear Father," and I. Cor. 16:22, "Maran atha;" that is, "The Lord cometh."

The historians tell us that when Noah had left the ark, his descendants multiplied and spread out in *Shinar*. This Shinar is Chaldea, and the language which has been spoken from ancient times to the present is the Chaldean. Then after the languages became confused at Babel the Hebrew began to exist; for that language appears first after that time.

The Hebrews are descended from Heber, the grandson of Arphaxad, and in particular from Abraham; but in his (Abraham's) time there already existed the Egyptian, as well as the Syrian, kingdom. A number of passages in the Bible bear witness to the fact that Canaan was already densely populated at a time when the Hebrews constituted only a small tribe. When Abraham withdrew from Ur of Chaldea and came to the "Promised Land," many Canaanites dwelt there; and when he came back out of Egypt, "the Persians inhabited the land." Furthermore the whole of the history of Abimeleck, the war of the four kings with the five, the mention of the cities of

Sodom and Gomorrah and their inhabitants, all indi-
cate a dense population at that time, and that this
period is far separated from the time of the confusion of tongues. But the Hebrews were a particular
branch, which now for the first time made its appearance in history.

Soon after the death of Abraham the Arabian
language grew up among the descendants of Elam
and Ishmael.

The Syrians were heathens, and were for this
reason called Arameans by the Jews, just as also to-
day Christians call all who are not Christians by the
universal name of heathen. But the ancestors of
Abraham on the farther side of the Euphrates were
likewise heathen; for God first called Abraham out
from among the heathen. It is quite possible that in
the time of the Bible prophets, God's word penetrated
here and there into Chaldea; as, for example, to Nineveh through the instrumentality of Jonah, to Damascus through Elisha, to Assyria through Nahum,
to Babylon through Ezekiel, Daniel, and other such
men of God. If we take into consideration the number of the heathen and their debasement, it is apparent that such individual efforts could not have
effected more than a drop of water upon a hot rock,
until the Messiah came to deliver his people. We
read in the history of the world that a Syrian king
had received the news that a great prophet had risen
up in Palestine, of whom many wonders were related;
as, for example, the raising of the dead, etc. Then

he sent messengers to him (Josephus records the letter), and requested him to come to Syria and heal his son, who was lying very ill, and also himself. But as Jesus was employed where he was, he could not go, and in person accommodate the king; but he sent to him two of his apostles, Thaddeus and Thomas (so says church history) in order that they might heal the sick boy. And they performed also still other wonders, raised the dead, and preached the new doctrine of life. Then this king and many Syrians with him believed; and the number of those who turned to Christ continually increased, and finally drove out the heathens. Then the Apostle Thomas returned to Palestine; but Thaddeus remained, and preached the gospel furtner. After a short time, Thaddeus and Abgar sent interpreters to Palestine to translate the Bible into the Syriac language. There began the Peshito, the old Syriac translation of the Bible; as also the historian Bar Hebræus relates in a part of his history. Since this time, the Syrians wear the name *Thomas Christians*; because indeed this apostle had stood in close relation to them, and had brought the gospel to them. So asserts *Hassan Bar Bahlul*, who was himself an Aramean, that the Syrians had originally been called Arameans. Then they took up the name Chaldeans, and finally they were called Thomas Christians.

At the time that Stephen was stoned at Jerusalem (Acts vii.) a fierce persecution arose against the apostles and believers; so they had to flee from the city.

The greater part of the fugitives took themselves to
Judea and Samaria, and a large number also came to
Antioch. There they spread the doctrine of life,and
many became believers. At the same time a church
of Christians was established in Antioch. But the
people of Antioch were of the Syrian race, and used
their language. (Acts 11:26.) The New Testament
was translated into the Syriac in the end of the first
century; and it is certain that the version called the
Peshito is the same as that which those sent by
Thaddeus and Abgar had made, with the exception
of the letter to the Hebrews, the three letters of John,
and the Revelation of John; for these books were not
in existence. They are first found inserted in the
Peshito of Mar Ephriam, in the fourth century. The
same however, indicates that the original is much older.

After the apostles, there preached among the
Syrians Mar Babay, Mar Maray, and Mar Edday,
and Christianity gained more and more ground. It
was then that the unbelieving Jews began to call the
believers Nazarenes, because the parents of Jesus
were of Nazareth. They were, and still are, called
Nazarenes by the Mohammedans of those regions.
In the church history we read of the great progress
of Christianity among Jews and heathens; and these
are largely indebted to the Syrians, for about the
year 340 the Syrian Church sent its missionaries to
the lands of the East, to Persia, Tartary, India, etc.
This missionary work continued till the year 1100. We
read about it in the Syrian history of the evangelists.

These missionaries, plain men with love and zeal for the cause, left their homes and pursued their way, often on foot and for months at a time. They went from place to place, with staff in hand, sandals on their feet, and a wallet on their backs. In this way they proceeded by the shores of the Persian Gulf, the Gulf of Omar, and the Arabian Sea, even to Persia and India, sowing the seed of the kingdom. Everywhere they left traces of their activity in the congregations of Christians they established.

In the sixth century the Syrians had twenty-five great seminaries of learning in various parts of Asia, some of the different countries being as follows: Elam, Mesopotamia, Arabia, Seleucia, Salamis, Persia, Khorassan, Hindostan, Armenia, Tartary, etc. Through the students of these schools the gospel seed had been sown in all the Eastern country. The first university was at Edessa, built by Mar Ephraim, and intended for the education of Syrians and heathens. It was destroyed by the Emperor Zenoo in 489. In Nesibia, Mar Nersay established a school in 490; King Agag one in Seleucia; two were in Bagdad, etc. In 832 the students at the school of Nesibia studied theology, astronomy, geometry, music, medicine, etc., three years.

The names of the best known missionaries may here be mentioned. They are Sheekah, Loshoa, Java, Laha, Thomas, Simus, Simon, Ephraim, Ananias, David, Barsheba, Johannes, Chilias, etc.

In the year 636 we hear of a missionary in China

by the name of Javalla, or Olopun, who preached the gospel forty-five years there. At the same time seventy other missionaries were working there. The history of them, together with an account of their labors, we find upon a stone which has been preserved. The writing on it is in both Syriac and Chinese languages, and was prepared in the time of the Emperor *Kien Chung.* English missionaries found the stone, and made photographs of it. One of them says: "I have seen the stone with my own eyes; the names of the missionaries are written upon it in the Syrian tongue; namely, Mar ——, Mar Thematias, Mar Javallaha, Mar Adam, etc." Then there is written, "Aquin kecisa, chura, episcopa, papisu be Sin Masan"—that is, "Make a preacher, a superior preacher, a bishop, a father in China."

In the year 1100 a Mongolian prince, Augh Kahn, with 200,000 men from his kingdom, accepted Christianity. These were all baptized by two preachers and deacons whom the Syrian patriarch had sent for that purpose. Augh Kahn, according to his own wish, took the name John. In the year 1103 Genghis Khan was married to the daughter of this John. She was an earnest Christian, and instructed her four sons in Christianity.

In the year 1300 Tamerlane, a Mussulman prince from Astrachan, in Russia, came to India in order to destroy the Christians in these regions by force of arms; he destroyed a great number of their churches, burnt their books, etc. He also waged war in China

for about twenty years. He was a vehement enemy
of Christianity. In 1502 the Patriarch Mar Elijah
sent four bishops to India and China, in order that
they might see with their own eyes, from the stand-
point of the churches, this great destruction. Their
names were Thomas, Javallaha, Dincha, and Jacob.
There is a record of a persecution of the churches in
China in the year 1540.

In the year 1541 the above-named patriarch sent
two bishops to India. At that time there were about
35,000 families of Christians in Ceylon and Malabar.
A great danger then threatened Christianity in the
Mohammedan religion, which since 1380 began to
take hold in India, and to spread more and more, until at last it became dangerous for Christians in the
East, just as in the West the rule of the Pope made
it dangerous to Protestants.

Let us again return to the Syrian Church in Asia
Minor. After the Councils of Nice and Constantinople, the church of the Greek Catholics, and also
the Roman Catholics, were very desirous that the
Syrian Church should unite with them into a great
whole. But the Syrians did not yield to them. They
held fast the belief of their ancestors, just as these
had received it from the apostles; and they declined
to make any concession whatever. From this time
came the hatred of the Western toward the Syrian
Church.

A patriarch in Constantinople by the name of
Nestorius, claimed openly at the Council of 428 that

he was opposed to the projected combination with the Greeks. He denied Mary's motherhood of God, and claimed that Mary was only the mother of the beloved Jesus. There he saw that he was very near to the belief of the Syrians. So he associated himself with them. This gave the Western churches the occasion to give the Syrian churches the name Nestorians, through hatred.

In the years 486–640 the Syrians were under the sway of the Persians. Sometimes they had rest from persecutions, but they were many times followed with unexampled persecutions. In particular, the Persian King, Techavur, was a mighty oppressor of Christianity, and shed the blood of believers. Among others, he had seven sons of a widow killed with a sword before the eyes of their mother, who encouraged them to be firm in their faith, and exhorted them to take refuge in Christ; and last of all, he had the mother herself killed. Afterward Mar Simon Bar Sabbay, according to the concurrent testimony of many Syrian books a very learned man, was witness of many persecutions of Christians, and himself a martyr.

The Syrian Christians came under the rule of the Mohammedan Arabians in the year 640. Mahomet had before his death sent a letter to the Syrian patriarchs, in which he commended them to the care of the believers; but these believers (Mussulmans) soon became a great number, and, as in the North the Greeks and Romans, so in the South the Saracens and Arabians, persecuted the poor Christianized

Syrians. Robbery and murder were a part of the daily order, and those who were left fled in all directions. A well-known poet says:

"Hasten and flee from place to place; only do not lose your faith; and wherever you come, bring also your treasure of life."

Thus the Syrians wandered by degrees away from their home, and finally reached the mountains of Kurdistan, just as the German Waldenses were compelled to seek shelter in the Alps. So the Syrians in the East, and the Waldenses in the West, had preserved a living Christian spirit, in a time when, on every hand, only an apparent Christianity subsisted, and when the truth of the Christian teaching was in danger of being destroyed by sundry foul and worldly customs. And both had to suffer alike under persecutions, the latter from the Pope, and the former from the Mohammedans.

In the beginning of the Arabian rule at Bagdad, in 762, a patriarch fled to Azerbijan in Persia, on the east of the Salt Sea; but here he still found no rest. He then betook himself to Urumiah, without here being able to get a firm foothold, like Noah's dove. At last he went to the mountains of Kurdistan. The residence of the patriarch is there to-day, in a hamlet called Kutschanis. The patriarchate is hereditary, and comes down to the son; but where the patriarch remains unmarried, to the son of his brother. The patriarch of that time was called Simon Peter; the one of the present, Reuben.

In the year 600 there came about a division of the Syrian Church. A very bold and eloquent man divided in some points of doctrine from the Syrian Church, and came nearer and nearer to the Roman. His followers were called Jacobites, and they continued to dwell to the south and east of Lebanon. In the year 713 a certain Maro appeared, whose doctrine inclined more toward the Greek Church. His followers were called Maronites.

At this time there were about 700,000 Thomas Christians in Syria and Southern India, in Madras and Malabar; but 500 years later the Roman Catholics came to this place, and sowed tares among the wheat of the Syrian Church.

Even to-day there are Thomas Christians in India; but their belief is no longer pure, as it is a mixture of Catholicism and Christianity. Also in Syria proper, some congregations have united with the Roman Church. People are given to designating them as Chaldeans. They live in Mosoul, Bagdad, Alkosel, Til Kipi, etc.

Of that great old Syro-Christian Church, there remain to-day only about 250,000 true Christians. Thirty-five thousand Syrians still dwell in the northern part of the kingdom of Persia. They hold firmly to the faith of their ancestors, although they are not learned, and have made little progress in understanding their holy books. The Syrians who settled in Kurdistan dwell between the inhabitants of Kurdistan and the Persians. The first are Sunnites, the latter are Shiites — that is, the inhabitants of Kurdistan recognize Saar, Omar, Abubekr, etc. The two sects are in continual hostility to each other, although they are agreed in the observance of the doctrines of the Koran. The Syrians have settled in many places of Kurdistan, as Kutschanis, Mar Bishoo, Baaz, El Bak, Suldooz, etc. The Syrians in Azerbijan live in Urumiah, Salamis, Somay, Tergava, etc. A small division also dwells in Russian Erivan. These are some who fled from Mohammedan persecutions at sometime, and have received the Russian confession. The Syrians in Iran (Persia), on the contrary, have shown themselves immovable under all foreign influences, although they are hedged in by the Mohammedan world. Emigrations to Russia continue to this day; but of course only in secret and in flight, for the Persian government gives no permission.

In consequence of all these persecutions the Syrian nation is rendered very poor, so that they are unable to give attention to teachers, books, and schools. The churches also are exposed to continued opposition; for the Persian government is intolerant toward them. The church buildings have also been exposed to continual devastation. A very old church building in Urumiah, St. Maria, was forcibly converted into a mosque by the Mohammedans; as had been the temple in Jerusalem, and St. Sophia in Constantinople. This is the great mosque still to be seen in Urumiah, and known by the name of the Mosque of Friday. The Sy-

rian Christians made their church-house doors
very low and small, so that only one at a time can
enter, in order that the Mohommedans may not
bring their horses into the church and hitch them.
Oftentimes also the Syrians have taken refuge from
their pursuers in the stone churches, for they could
close the doors and save themselves and their families
from pursuit.

But the Syrians are not yet destroyed from the
face of the earth, though not on account of pity on
the part of the Mohammedan, but self-interest; for he
is their master, and they are to him like the sheep
and the ox which are kept and protected only for the
sake of their work, and flesh, and hides.

The doctrine of Islam does not permit its followers to traffic with those of another faith in such
things as butter, cheese, bread, flesh, fruits, etc. And
now that our emperor, judge, governor, and our mas-
ters are all Mohammedans, the Christian, if he be
never so full of integrity and devotion to God, if he is
a preacher or a bishop, has no value before a court.

It has for a long time been a fact that we have
been forced to see beautiful wives and young girls
compelled by force to submit to Mohammedanism;
and it is still more notorious that, when one of them
thus by force marries a Syrian maiden, all remon-
strance, or attempt at redress on the part of her parents, is vain.

The present condition of the Syrians is such that
they cannot even become merchants, etc., for the

foregoing reasons. In agriculture they sow, they
reap, and prepare the grain to bring to their master,
who keeps two-thirds of it, and leaves them, after all
their pains, only one-third. And in addition to this,
permission to cultivate the fields must be purchased
by a special tax. Such hardness and cruelty are not
to be found elsewhere in all the world. By such
means the Persians continue to hold the Syrians as
serfs; and they call them *Kaffir*, a name which has
been handed down to them from the time of the
heathen fire-worshippers.

We have the European States, which keep ambassadors or consuls there, to thank very much and very
heartily; because they have for a long time given us
their protection. And we are under obligations to
them for other favors also; for sixty years ago we had
only twenty New Testaments, three Bibles, and a
part of the Psalms of David, and in addition to this
35,000 tracts. But even these books existed only in
the old Syriac language, in manuscript. Now, by
the kindness of the Europeans, we have books
printed in the new Syriac language. We also have
in our possession about one hundred and fifty manu-
scripts of good instruction in religious matters; but
they are in the Old Syriac, and not generally
understood.

Our people have been like the Israelites were in
Egypt. Because of oppressions they had not time
to seek God; but were driven onward in the labors
of the field.

We were not permitted to put bells in our churches, because the Mohammedan might be disturbed in his worship by the ringing of the bells. So, for a bell, we had a wooden board, perforated with holes, which was repeatedly struck. In the villages, where there were no churches, a man ran out early in the morning and cried, "Kummschobchan Solabschan," *i. e.*, "Pray to your God." And the people worshipped at this signal.

When the Sheik of Kurdistan, Ibad Illak, determined to make himself king of Persia, he came to Urumiah with fifty thousand men. He was a very cruel man, fearing neither God nor man. He burned villages and killed many Mohammedans, and about one hundred Christians. He took away five wives and daughters of Christians as prisoners. He robbed young and old of their clothing, beds, etc. It was the old question of the Sunnites and the Shiites, which had come here again in an outbreak, and partially spent its force upon the heads of the Christians.

Now our people are greatly in need of the blessed gospel; and not only our nation, but the many different nations in Persia are all in need of it. The door is now open, and the great need is laborers. Preachers bearing the word will be received gladly everywhere. Our many different people are like sheep without a shepherd. The Christians are the instruments in the hands of God to save his people from their sins. So our duty is to look for, and take care of, everyone, to bring him to Christ.

Daniel 12:3: "And they that be wise shall shine as the brightness of the firmament; and they that turn many to righteousness, as the stars forever and ever."

James 5:20: "Let him know, that he which converteth the sinner from the error of his way shall save a soul from death, and shall hide a multitude of sins."

There are many examples of such conversions as this, although we give only one below.

Only twenty months ago, Mirza Ibrahim made the assertion, under severe pain, even under death tortures, "I am a Christian."

He was baptized at Choi, in the northwestern province of Aserbeidsham, in 1889. It was known by him that the Mohammedans' law was to punish severely those who became Christians; still he did not hesitate, and was baptized publicly.

At first he was not disturbed by the Mohammedans, but soon the hatred of these fanatical people rose against him. He had to flee for safety, going to Urumiah, where he lodged with the Syrian preacher, David. This came to the ears of the Khan, and he then commanded David to drive Ibrahim from his house. David would not do this, so the Khan had them both come before him. The judge asked Ibrahim what his religion was. The latter, holding a New Testament in his hand, said that what he held in his hand was the gospel, and he was a Christian. He was next asked what he thought about Mahomet. The answer was, "That is your business; I have spoken my belief." The command then came, "Strike him," and an attack was made upon him; even the judge seized upon him. They were, after trial, cast into prison. But the word of God was not bound; he preached to the willing hearers in the prison. When attacks were made upon the prison, to take him and slay him, he said: "They can bind me before a cannon's mouth, but they can not make me turn from my faith in Christ."

After many such trials and persecutions as these, he was taken to Tabris. In this place, also, as in the other, he suffered from almost innumerable persecutions. They cast him into prison and chained him with robbers and murderers. Their manner of chaining is as follows: The prisoners are bound together in groups of ten or twelve each. Iron bands are bound about their necks, and then they are all bound together by a long iron chain. Ibrahim asked his friends to send him a piece of matting to spread on the prison floor, for he had to lie among worms and vermin. But, according to the goodness of God, he was soon freed from the large chains.

As in the other prison, so in this he preached the gospel, by this means moving deeply some of his fellow-prisoners. They tempted him again and again, but he was still immovable, until at last he was killed, rejoicing to take his departure and be with his Master.

The death of Mirza Ibrahim has again laid a

breach in the walls of Mohammedanism. They did not believe that the followers of Mahomet could be induced to turn away to Christianity. So, when they saw such a thing take place, they bought New Testaments to read and see what kind of doctrine it teaches.

We need no longer to ask God to open the doors to the Mohammedans; they are wide open. Let us pray for great strength and courage to enter in at the open doors.

May it be God's will that the gospel may go to those people, is my prayer.

CHAPTER VII.

ARMENIANS.

This book treats generally of Persia, but probably the reader would like to know something about the Armenians. Though I have been reared among them, I will quote part of Dr. Barton's "Turkey and Armenia." According to Armenian history, the first chief of the Armenians was Haik, the son of Torgomah, the son of Gomar, the son of Japheth, the son of Noah. In fact, the Armenians of to-day call themselves Haik, their language "Haioren, and their country Haiasdon." The name Armenia was given to them and their country by the outside nations, because of one of their kings, Arom, the seventh from Haik. Probably this people is composed of the Aryan tribes, who conquered the country now occupied by the Armenians. They have had a long line of kings of bravery and renown; they were an independent nation, but with various degrees of power' until A. D., 1375, when they became completely a subject people. Since that time the country has been under the government of Russia, Persia, and Turkey. From 600 B. C., to about 400 A. D., this nation played a prominent part in the wars of the Assyrians, Medes, Persians, Turks, and Romans. There are probably about 4,000,000 Armenians in Turkey, Persia, and Russia; but as no separate record is kept, we must be content with an estimate

based upon mere observation and inadequate government returns.   In no extended district do they com-
prise a majority of the inhabitants, but are everywhere mixed and surrounded by Kurds and Turks.
The Armenians are forbidden, under a severe penalty,
to carry or possess any arms, while all the other
races are armed, many of them by the government.
Armenian histories state that soon after the resurrection of Christ, Abdar, the king of Armenia, with his
court, accepted Christianity; but in the third century, A. D., under the leadership of Gregory, the
Armenian people, as a nation, became Christians.
This was the first nation to adopt Christianity as a
national religion.   The church was called Gregorian
(illuminator).   The Gregorians and Greeks worked
in harmony in the great councils of the church until 451 A. D., at the fourth Ecumenical council,
which met at Chalcedon that year.   The Gregorian
church then separated from the Greek church, upon
the so-called monophysite doctrine.   The former accepted it and the latter rejected it.   Since then the
Gregorian church has been distinctly and exclusively
an Armenian National church.

The organization and control is essentially Epis-
copal, and the spiritual head is Catholic; but in addition to this head is, the Patriarch, whose office
bears largely on the political life as related to the
Ottoman government.   There are nine grades of
Armenian clergy, three of them residing, in the
order of their importance, at three different places.

The Bible was translated into their language about
the middle of the fifth century, but, owing to a
change in the spoken language, it became a dead
book. Though it was constantly read in their church
services, yet, even the priest himself, seldom understood what the Scripture meant.

Christian doctrine was kept alive by oral teaching; but the restraint upon life, which pure religion
exercises, was largely removed. They blindly accepted the Bible as the word of God. There are
many fine churches, some of which are several hundred years old. This nation has suffered great persecution for its faith during the last eleven centuries,
but with wonderful patience it has clung to its old
belief and form of worship. Missionary work was
first begun among them for the purpose of introduc-
ing the Bible in their spoken language, in order that
its teaching might reform the church and the nation.
The Armenian nature is essentially religious; the
customs, traditions, and teachings of religion have
great influence over their lives. Although much of
their teachings and many of their customs are based
upon mere traditions, and are not in accord with the
enlightened Christianity of other nations, neverthe-
less, during the last three years, thousands of them
have deliberately chosen death and terrible torture,
rather than to worship Islam. This shows that
among them there exists much essential Christian
faith. It must not be overlooked that the old church
has been greatly educated and enlightened by the

Missions. The Armenians are the most intelligent of all people that inhabit the country; they far outstrip their Mohammedan rulers in desire for a liberal education, and in their ability to attain to a genuine scholarship. This nation has produced many well-known scholars. These facts, taken together with the general high scholarship among her students, and the eager desire prevalent among the people for a liberal education, show that the race, intellectually, compares favorably with the most enlightened nations of the world. The Armenians are the farmers, artisans, tradesmen, and bankers of eastern Turkey and Persia. They have strong commercial instincts, mature ability, and, being industrious, they have made much progress in all these lines in spite of the heavy restrictions placed upon them by the Turkish government in the form of general regulations and excessive taxes. In some parts of Turkey and Persia the leading business operations are largely in their hands.

The industrious Armenian takes readily to a new trade. When in a foreign country, he easily adapts himself to new surroundings, and does creditable service in almost any line of work. This adaptability, together with the tendency to hold to a trade once begun, has given a stable character to the nation. The Armenian is domestic in his habits and aspirations, rather than military. In the early history of the race we do not find much written of their conquests, since they did not go outside of their borders, as a general thing, to conquer their neighbors. Their chief ambition appears to have been to possess their beloved fatherland, "Hairenik," where they might worship God according to the demands of their own church. To-day, they have no desire for conquest or ambition to rule; their greatest wish is to be able to enjoy, without fear, the blessings of their simple domestic life, together with the privilege of worship and education, and the opportunity to possess, in peace, the fruits of their frugal industry. The Armenian loves his children, and is most closely attached to his home. When he emigrates, it is only for the purpose of trade and gain. His heart's affection centers in the old rude home, to which, if not prevented, he will return again. The city or village of his birth is the dearest spot on earth to him.

The Armenians are most simple in their manner of life, uncomplaining, and generally cheerful. They continue their occupation without any desire for a change: the son of a carpenter is a carpenter, and the shoemaker sticks to his last, without a thought of being anything else so long as that trade makes him a living. The home life, as in all Eastern countries, is patriarchal, the father ruling the household. The sons bring their wives to the paternal roof. In the event of the death of the father, the oldest son takes his place at the head of the family. The aged are held in high esteem, and their counsel sought and honored.

The Armenian women, as a class, are ignorant,

but, as a rule, they are industrious. Their features are regular and they are handsome. Their costume differs from that of the Moslem women. It consists of long, flowing skirts, worn both indoor and out, and the head is wrapped very closely at all times. They are married by their parents at the age of twelve. Their marriage and betrothal ceremonies vary considerably from that of the Mohammedans, although both are performed by the priest. As among nearly all Orientals, the wife is considered the inferior of her husband in every respect. Women are not allowed to talk loudly or freely in the presence of men, the *pashmak*, or mouth covering, being almost as strict and binding as among the Moslems.

Those of them who have not been reached by the Protestant missionaries are very low in their morals; outbroken profanity is often heard. They believe in Jesus Christ and the Bible, yet they depend entirely upon the priest to read and interpret the scriptures for them; their understanding is sadly darkened, and their ideas so paganish that it might truly be said of them, when unevangelized: "They have a name to live while they are dead." That God may open the hearts of His children to send fire-baptized, full-salvation preachers to this people, is my prayer.

Armenians are superstitious, as all other Oriental people, concerning the birth of a child. These superstitions are of a vague and indefinite character. If possible, a mother and child are not left alone the first few days; the broom is replaced by the venerated

image of the holy virgin, or some holy saint that is
put on guard over the bed; garlic is not resorted to
as a safeguard against the evil eye, but holy water is
sprinkled nightly over the child and mother, who are
also fumigated with the holy olive branch; the company received on these occasions is quiet. About the
ninth day the bath ceremony takes place; they provide food for the guests, and it is brought into the
bathroom on this occasion. As the christening takes
place within eight days, it can not be witnessed by
the mother, who is unable to attend the church service before the fortieth day, when she goes to receive
the benediction of purification. Some of the water
used for the christening is presumably brought from
the river Jordan.

On this occasion the child is rubbed with holy
oil.   When the service is concluded the company
walk home in a procession, headed by the mid-wife
carrying the baby; refreshments are offered to the
company, who soon afterwards retire. A gift of a
golden cross, or of a fine gold coin is made to the
child by the sponsors. No system of diet is followed
in the rearing of Armenian children, neither are
their bodies refreshed by baths. Few people in the
East bathe their children, for a general idea pre-
vails that bathing causes sickness. They are allowed
to struggle through infancy in a very irregular manner, yet, in spite of all this, they are healthy. My
dear reader, it seems to me your heart should be
touched for the millions of precious souls in foreign

lands dying without Jesus in their hearts. God move you, is my prayer.

> "Christ is coming! Let creation
> Bid her groans and travail cease;
> Let the glorious proclamation
> Hope restore and faith increase;
> Christ is coming!
> Come, thou blessed Prince of Peace."

REV. B. L. SARMAST AND WIFE.

CHAPTER VIII.

WOMAN IN PERSIA.

This chapter will be interesting to the ladies who wish to know about the women of other countries. To know them best, we must begin at babyhood. The baby life of a girl in Persia is not more than two years, which is the limited time for nursing a baby. The time may be reduced to twenty-one months, but anyone who goes below that is guilty of a "gross misdemeanor." The birth of a child is usually awaited with a great deal of agonizing anxiety. At the announcement of the birth of a baby boy the servants have a glorious time. They joyfully take the tidings to their master, from whom they are certain to receive gifts, and hear good words. The congratulations of friends and relatives will begin to pour in from all quarters to the happy father, and it will be an occasion for rejoicing and festivity. The father will deem it a privilege to entertain his friends as an expression of his personal gratification. Noise, festivity and music will fill the air with echoes of a merry company. Everybody is happy because a son is born: one who will succeed the father, keep up the family record, and perpetuate the memory of the race.

But when a daughter is born there will be no giving of gifts, no festivity, no music and no entertainment. Everything about the house, even the very atmosphere, will be doleful and gloomy, as though the mourning for the loss of a precious child were already begun. The servants dread to take the tidings to their master, realizing the disappointment that will follow. When the father hears the message, he will be in a woeful condition. Taking his pipe, he will engage in an endless puffing, as though thus to mitigate his sorrow. The mother's grief is most sincere and pitiful. She weeps bitterly when her friends come to her with comforting words and encouraging prospects. Both the mother and infant will be the object of hatred to the cruel father and the rest of the family. No word of comfort will be given to her by them; no kiss of affectionate love, and no help in the time of pain and sorrow.

It is the custom on the wedding day for the friends of the married couple to express their good wishes by repeating the common saying: "May your wedded life be long and peaceful, with many sons, and one daughter." The birth of a daughter is supposed to be a calamity.

According to an ancient custom, the child is salted on the day that she is born, and subjected to all the superstitions so carefully practiced among their women. If it is a boy, none can see his face for at least three months, because the little fellow is so precious that, peradventure anyone should look upon him he might die. A talisman will soon be brought, on which are written prayers and verses from the Koran. This is to be fastened to his right arm, or put somewhere near him, to preserve him from sickness, and from the evil eye. But the unfortunate little daughter will have no more attention, at first, than a domestic animal. At the end of seven days she will be put in a hard cradle, wrapped tightly in swaddling clothes. Sometimes she is not removed from the cradle for a whole day and night; and when she is removed, it will be for only a little while. When she cries, the mother is slow to attend to her; and at last, the only thing the mother will do for her when she cries, is to rock her in the rough cradle which does not add much to her comfort, nor soothe her into silence. After a considerable amount of rocking and singing and harsh speaking, very likely the mother will get tired and angry, (she needs religion) and leave the little creature alone to cry until it can cry no longer, because utterly exhausted. At night it is even worse.

As to the father, months will pass before he will take even a distant look at his little daughter's face. Such is the condition of the daughters among the masses.

The Naming of a Child.

As circumcision is universally practiced among the Mohammedans, boys receive their names at the celebration of this rite when they are seven or eight days old. But at the naming of girls, there is no religious ceremony, and no reading of the Koran, nor even praying by the Mollah, (Priest). An old woman will be called to the house. She will take the ten days old girl in her arms, and, putting her mouth to the child's ear, will call the name in a very loud voice; repeating it three times and adding: "This is your name." This is the way the little girl gets her name.

Persian feminine names are very pretty, and always have a meaning. Some of their names are "Almos," (diamond), "Shireen" (sweet), "Voohahor" (spring), "Shomsi" (the sun), "Gulshan" (lilies), etc. As they have no family names, every girl retains her own sweet maiden name all through her life.

The child life of a girl in Persia usually begins when the baby is weaned, and lasts until she is six or seven years old. Thus, you see, in Persia, childhood is of very short duration as compared with that of girls in America or any other civilized country. It is of vital and infinite importance that adequate opportunities should be provided for the mental and moral, as well as the physical, development of the child; and herein lies the responsibility of parents. To understand better their situation, we give a few important points concerning the child-life of a girl.

The first thing is the play-room, which is absolutely wanting in Persia. There is no place in the house where children may freely play. A Persian mother will not permit it, because she dislikes the noise; and she is too lazy to clear away the dirt and disorder they are sure to make. As they cannot play at home, they are obliged to go out of doors, to the streets, where they can do as they please: or if they prefer to stay at home, they must be silent and motionless; else they will be pretty sure of punishment.

Another thing is that this little girl needs training. But girls get no training whatever in manners and habits, and the boys not much more. The mothers will not take the trouble to teach them anything until they are obliged to, and as they are not associated with grown people at that age, either in the dining-room or parlor, they know little of table or society manners. They have opportunity on the streets to learn only vulgar language, profanity, stealing, and lying; for which they are not punished, the parents rather smiling at them, because they think it is smart. (It was this way with the author until he reached the age of thirteen.) Another very important thing is the neglect of the religious training of the child. The Mohammedan idea of the soul, or the religious life of a child, is very degrading. They believe that until a girl has passed her fourteenth year, there is no use to teach her, or read to her anything concerning religion, while the Christian mother begins, as soon as the little girl can speak, to teach her the sweet prayer, "Now I lay me down to sleep," and to lead her thoughts up to God. You can easily believe that there is no happy child-life in Persia, as says the great lady traveler, Mrs. Bishop, after some experience of home life in Persia.

The maiden life of a girl in Persia begins at the age of eight or nine, and ends when she is fifteen or

sixteen. During this period, every girl is supposed
to be at the proper age for marriage. Her life at this
time differs widely from that of a child. This is the
age of activity and preparation for the duties of life
and the relation of the mother to the daughter is
closer than before. The mother feels great concern
about the accomplishments and attainments of her
daughter; not so much, it must be confessed, from
increased affection, as from anxiety to make sure of
the maiden's being well married. In the beginning
of this period, they are closely confined at home. At
the age of eight they will be put to work at home
helping their mothers, and at the same time learning
what will be useful to themselves. They are taught
sweeping, washing, cooking, etc.

The Education of the Maiden.

There are no schools for girls in Persia, because
education is not considered essential to the training
of a woman. They do not believe that a woman is fit
to have an education. Should any one suggest to a
father to send his daughter to school, he would shrug
his shoulders and say: "Why, shall I make her a
priest?" Once a missionary asked a Moslem to send
his daughter to a mission school. He replied in a
very astonished way: "Educate a girl! why you
might as well attempt to educate a cat!" Now, what
can these poor daughters and wives do, when their
own fathers and husbands speak thus of them? This
is always the case with Mohammedans.

The Wedded Life of a Girl.

Thus women, although secluded and debased, are yet the central figures upon whom every eye is fixed. A man can put himself under no greater curse than to choose a poor bachelor's life. On the other hand, marriage is supposed to be the whole destiny of a girl. To be an old maid is something sinful, hateful, and absolutely out of the question. In fact, there is no word in the Persian to denote "bachelor." The prophet said, "Marry, and establish a family." The most wicked among the dead are the unmarried persons. According to Mohammedanism, there is no greater benefit to a man than to have a Mussulman wife who pleases his eye, obeys him, and, in his absence, watches faithfully over his honor and his goods.

The Betrothal.

For the girl, the common age of betrothal is between ten and twelve years of age. Very seldom over that, but in a great many cases a girl is betrothed as soon as she is born; or even before her birth. I have known men who were friends before their marriage, to make an agreement that, after they were married, if one had a daughter and the other a son, they would marry them to each other. In Kurdistan the girls are sold as soon as they are born.

There is a certain ceremonial, beginning after the parents of the boy have made up their minds as to whom they desire their son to be betrothed. They first send a private message to the father of the girl, indicating their wishes. If her father favors the idea, he will return words of encouragement, and the date of the ceremony will then be fixed. Then the father of the boy, with a few of his relatives, takes a ring, a pair of shoes, a head dress, and some pieces of money, usually from five to ten coins (Luke 15:8-10), with a great deal of candy, meat, rice, etc., and goes to the home of the girl. After an elaborate salutation, they will be given seats, and there will be a general conversation. Then the father of the boy will mention the object of his coming, addressing the family in a few appropriate words. The father of the girl, who is expected to decide the matter, at first will say, "The girl does not belong to me, she has a grandfather who must be consulted first." Then the grandfather will be pressed for an answer, and he will place the matter before the girl's uncle; and so it will go the round of all the nearest relatives. After all have been consulted, it comes back to the father of the girl again, and the definite answer will be like this: "My daughter is like a pair of shoes for your son." That means that he is willing for the betrothal. Then it is the duty of the father of the boy to get up and kiss the hand of every relative of the girl who is present. Meantime the ring will be carried by an elderly woman to the ladies' apartment, where the girl is. In addressing her, the woman will say: "Your father, and your

uncle, etc., have betrothed you to so and so, and if
you are willing to obey them, you may express it by
taking this ring from my hand and putting it on
your finger." And the girl is always expected to do
this. Then the presents will be offered, and the
feasting will begin, coutinuing until a late hour in
the night. Thus the engagement is solemnized, and
is as binding as real marriage. The duration of
betrothal varies greatly. Some marry in five months,
while others wait three or four years. During this
period, the girl is not allowed to go on the street, or
to show her face in any public place.

The boy rarely gets to see his future wife, even
from a distance. There is no calling on sweethearts,
nor walking with them, nor any pleasant association
together. It is considered improper for a girl to
allow her sweetheart to see her. It is customary during this period, on any important festival or national
day, and at different seasons of the year, for the
family of the boy to take appropriate gifts to the
girl. For example, on the great day of "Narus,"
New Year's Day, which comes on the 14th of March,
seven kinds of confectionery and fruits are used in
feasting, and these must be taken to the young
betrothed. In addition, a quantity of oil, and rice,
and often a dressed sheep are presented. When the
spring comes, they must take her spring fruits or
vegetables, and this has to be kept up until the wedding takes place. Neglect of these little attentions
will provoke a great deal of grumbling and discon-

tent on the part of the girl's people, and even in community.

Wedding Garments.

One of the special features of Persian weddings is this: from the time the engagement takes place until the wedding is over large sums of money are being spent by both parties; more especially by the bridegroom's family. The wealthy may not feel the pressure much, but there are some upon whom it brings a heavy burden of debt for life. Still they think it necessary, for a man's character and generosity are measured by the style in which he marries his son. The greatest expense is "parcha" (the wedding garments). Usually they buy from three to five suits for the bride, giving but small attention to the bridegroom. The expenses must be paid by the boy's parents

The wedding invitations are different from those engraved cards sent through the mail in America. Two or three days before the time appointed, the bridegroom's people will send some of their men to the villages and towns of the neighborhood, to invite all the friends, relatives, and respectable citizens. They carry with them candy and red apples, which are to take the place of engraved cards. Handing some candy or a red apple to the head of the family, they will announce the day of the wedding, adding these words: "Mr. and Mrs. B. send their love to you and your family, and say the wedding is not our son's,

but your son's. Come and bring your family." Then
bidding them farewell, they will go to the next neighbor and say the same thing, and so on until their
mission is fulfilled. (Matt. 22: 3.)

The weddings in Persia usually last from three
to seven days. On the first day, invited guests will
begin to come to the home of the bridegroom, which
is open for their cordial reception, and everyone
makes himself at home. The sound of dancing,
music, noisy drums, and the great excitement of
noisy crowds will fill the air. The first three days
are spent in feasting at the bridegroom's house, while
the bride's family are quietly going on with the
preparations for their daughter.

The principal part of the entertainment during
these days consists in eating. The home is thrown
open for not only the guests, but for all the poor people and the beggars. Sometimes from five to fifteen
sheep will be slain, or one or two oxen. (Matt. 22:4.)

Three times a day the crowd of people will sit on
the floor around the long tables to eat, of course
with their fingers, according to the custom of the
country. You will wonder how so many strangers
and guests from abroad can be accommodated at
night. It is customary for each neighbor who is
present at the supper table, to take from two to six
of them home with him and take care of them at
night. On the last day they arrange to go after the
bride. Some fifty or a hundred of the best young
men, well dressed and armed, and, if the bride's

home be at some distance, some of them mounted on beautiful horses, march to the town in which the bride lives. They will receive a cordial welcome. Everything has been prepared for their reception, and feasting will begin at the home of the bride. The next morning the bride will be dressed in her wedding apparel, in the women's apartment, a red veil covering the whole of her body. After bidding her relatives goodby, she is put upon a horse that has been saddled for her, and at this point begins a tremendous uproar from the crowd; yells, shouts, firing of guns, etc. The bride is carefully protected from every danger by three men, one holding the bridle and leading the horse, and the other two holding her, one on either side. The procession advances as rapidly as possible. When they are near the home of the bridegroom a messenger is sent to carry to him the news of their approach. The bridegroom dresses himself in his wedding costume, and goes out of his chamber with his intimate companions, stands upon the roof, and waits until the bride is a hundred yards away from the house. He has three apples in his hand, and kissing each one, he tries to throw it over the bride's head. When the apples strike the ground, there is a crowd of boys ready to scramble for them, for there is a superstition that any boy that catches the apple is lucky, and will be the next to marry.

Then the bride goes to her new home, and everybody will retire until next morning. The next day's proceedings will be the welcoming of the bride's rel-

atives and friends, who will come and bring her trunk
and all that belongs to her. Her trunk must be
opened before a multitude of witnesses, and every little thing that it contains spread out before them.
On the next day the guests will begin to depart. On
leaving, each one presents his or her congratulations,
and presents his or her gifts. This ends the wedding.
The married couple will do no work for three months,
but remain at home and take life easy, sometimes
visiting.

Polygamy.

It has been the cause of thousands of heart-
breaks as well as home-breaks, poisoning the happiness of races and nations as well as families, from
the time of Abraham to the present day. The Old
Testament tells us that the Persian kings in the
days of Esther practiced polygamy, which was
kept up by their descendants; but since the intro-
duction of Mohammedanism into the country, polygamy has been revived, and is taught in the Koran
(their Bible). In this book, Mahomet commanded
his followers to marry four wives and no more, but
the author has seen men that had been married to
forty wives. A priest told me that he was forty-three
years old, and he had been married forty-two times.
They give glory to God because they are allowed to
marry more than one. If anyone loves tall women,
he will marry tall ones. If he likes fat ones, he will
marry those. They also give glory to God that they
are not Christians, because they are not bound as a

slave to one woman, or one woman to one man. Beside all this, they are free to take as many fine slave girls as they wish.

Marriage Ceremony.

There are several kinds of marriages in Persia. "Ahda" (covenant) marriage must be legalized in the presence of a Mollah (priest) and two witnesses, one from the girl's side, and one from the boy's side. The Mollah writes a contract, which is called "Kabin," in which the full amount of the wife's portion is mentioned. The writing is given to the girl to keep, so that in the case of divorce she will be able by it to secure the amount that is allowed her in the contract.

The other kinds of marriages are called, "Sigah" (concubinage), and home exchange marriage, and temporary marriage. This last kind has been practiced by the travelers.

Divorce.

The divorce is at the option of the husband, for any reason, or without any reason. The cause may be sickness, or some other reason that will cause the divorce; but generally the man will divorce his wife for the sake of some other woman. Sometimes the jealousy of a new wife may cause the divorce. If a man in a fit of anger says, "You are divorced," divorce is not accomplished unless he repeats the words three times. He can recall a divorced wife without further ceremony, unless he has fully

divorced her the third time. If a husband divorces
his wife the third time, she is not lawful for him
again until she marries another husband. The
divorce is pronounced by the husband and wife in
the presence of three. The wife will say, "Kohinim
halal jonim kizad," which means, "I resign my portion in order that my soul may be free." Then she
is divorced. The man will say, "Entie jalakoon," *i. e.*,
"Thou art divorced." After divorce, women have to
wait three months and three days. During this period,
perhaps the divorced parties will marry again. If they
do not marry each other, then she is free to marry some
one else. The evil results of these marriage laws
are seen not only in women as individuals, but in
society as a whole. What would be thought in
America of a mother who would give away or sell
her little daughter of ten or twelve years? This is
what the mother of the child-wife in Mohammedan countries does. The little thing does not know
where she will go, nor what will be her future life.
And again it ruins their physical and intellectual development. Girls become mothers at an age when
they should be busy in securing knowledge and im-
proving themselves in every way possible. They are
also made subjects, and are dependent upon the men
for everything, and are treated as beasts of burden.
The outcome of this kind of marriage has been the
corruption of home and society. It brings envy,
jealousy and hatred, and has made the home a den of
misery instead of the abode of peace and love.

We have mentioned in the first chapter of this book the costumes of the women in Persia, the manner of dressing, etc. In the last part of this chapter we will show their occupation. In Persia no woman will be found in a shop, store, or any other market place. The Persians believe that "God made the women to stay at home." So the women are either at home doing nothing, or in some other place engaged in hard work. Of course there is a great difference between the wealthy and poor. The occupation of the wealthy women is very limited. They do very little or nothing, having servants for everything. They only eat, sleep, and smoke their water pipes. Some of them do a little sewing and spend most of the day in fancy work. They do not try, as the American women, to run for office. They would do so, but they cannot. On the other hand, the women of the lower classes are hard workers. Equal to the beasts of burden, besides the home work—such as cooking, cleaning and taking care of the little ones, they do out-door work—that is, haying, etc. Their time is occupied in hard toiling, with but little chance to rest. Some do not rest at all. One of the most important of their labors is grinding at the mill. They have to grind the wheat into flour, especially in those parts of Persia where water is scarce. Their mills are called horse, donkey, and mule mills. Some years ago the writer remembers a buffalo mill located near his home. In places where water is plentiful they build water mills; but there are so many poor people who cannot afford to have their wheat ground at these mills that the women must grind at home, and this is done in the old-fashioned way as it is spoken of in the Bible, Matt. 24:41. The mill consists of two circular stones with a wooden pin in the center fastened to the lower one and passing through a large hole in the upper one. Into this hole the grain is poured by the handful; and two women turn it rapidly by the handle, fastened to the outer rim of the upper stone. The grain, falling between these two stones, is crushed into a rough flour and thrown out around the mill, into a large cloth that is spread under the mill. Besides flour, this mill is used to make what is called cracked wheat, which is boiled in water with lard; this is greatly relished by Persians.

The women work also in vineyards. When the grapes are ripe, the women will gather large basketsful and carry them and spread them out in the sun to be dried into raisins. After they are dried they are gathered up and taken to their homes ready for sale. The remaining grapes are made into wine, whiskey, and molasses. The heaviest part of the work in the vineyard is done by the men.

The milking and churning are done by the women. The author remembers when he first saw men do the milking and churning in America. It seemed very strange indeed to him to see a man doing a woman's work. In the Oriental country such men are called women. In Persia the churning is done in a large earthen jar laid upon its side on a kind of

saddle made of wood. Upon this it is jolted back-
wards and forwards to separate the butter from the
milk.

There being no water wells or cisterns brings
another kind of hard work upon women. The water
is brought in earthen jars, that hold about ten gallons
of water, and are carried on their shoulders for a distance of half a mile or more. It is a beautiful sight
to see every morning many women going, with their
jars upon their backs, to the spring. This will re-
mind the reader of the stories that are told in Gen.
24, and John 4.

The sewing and making of clothes is done entirely
by women. All the clothing of men and women
must be made by hand, because there are not many
sewing machines there.

The hardest work of a Persian woman is harvest-
ing, which begins in the hottest season of the year—
the last of June—and lasts all July. The poor women
have to get up very early in the morning and do all
the house-work, then rush to the fields, there to labor
till dark. Often you will see one, with a cradle upon
her shoulder, having to go a distance of two or three
miles.

We have said very little about the work of women
in Persia. Their life is undoubtedly a hard one.
They cannot expect to have an easier life than this,
as it has been mentioned in some of the preceding
chapters that Persians look upon woman as an inferior being. There is no hope for the poor women

of that race, except in the religion of Jesus Christ.
That will make men love their wives as themselves
and look upon women as upon their own selves.

The Social Life in General.

The Persians generally are a very sociable people,
and kind, and very entertaining. They are very
much amused by stories and jokes. They are much
given to visiting and feasting.

The social intercourse of men and women is not
permitted. Men visit with men and women with
women. They sometimes have national holidays,
but they have a great many more religious feasts.
The greatest feast they have is the feast of the Naruz
(New Year). It is celebrated somewhat like Christmas
in America. The most beautiful time of the new year
is on March 14th. At that time the herbs begin to
spring out of their winter beds, the flowers to bud
and bloom very beautifully all over the country; and
this is the time that nature begins to put on its robe
of different colors of flowers, and the farmer takes
up his work in the fields. This festival is of very
ancient origin. There is no correct history of the
festival. It is not known who were the originators
of it, although the Persians have some traditions
concerning its origin. On this day almost everybody is happy — men, women, and children. For
several days before the great day comes, the heads of
families will go to the city and buy a variety of
fruits. These fruits must be of seven kinds, which

are called "Yedi-lamoon." Many send to their
friends a plate full, with the compliments of the
season. The last day is the greatest day. On the
evening of that day, every family has fire-crackers;
boys crowd the streets, and women the housetops, to
see the show; and there is a grand display of fire-
works from each housetop or street, so that the towns
and cities look as if they were on fire.

The Dervishes pitch their tents before the gates
of rich people and stay during the festival days.
Every day they recite poems and prayers until their
claims for charity are satisfied.

Generally, during these days, all Bazaars (markets)
are closed, and all business suspended. All are bent
on pleasure. It is the proper time to renew old
acquaintances, and to make new ones; to visit both
rich and poor. The social habit, which is so universally exemplified at Naruz, is a striking trait of the
Persian character. One of the social institutions of
great attraction is the tea-house. The tea-houses are
of various grades. Some are rudely furnished, with
a raised platform which surrounds the sides of the
room and is covered with matting or carpet. Others
have an air of comfort imparted to them by divans,
mirrors, chandeliers, etc. With the tea they have
common pipes, cigarettes, and the sooty Kalian
(water-pipe). The ordinary water-pipe is about two
feet and a half high. It consists of a vase or bottle
of glass holding a quart of water, with a picture
of the Shah (king) on the outside. Through the

narrow neck of this passes a wooden tube, reaching half-way down into the water, and extending some distance above the neck of the bottle, where it enters another vessel of brass, silver, or gold, richly ornamented. This is called the "head," and contains a little dampened tobacco with some pieces of burning charcoal on top of it. From this tube, just above the mouth of the lower vessel, is another tube, the mouth-piece or stem, about twenty inches long, through which the smoke passes through water, and is then drawn into the lungs. One of the water-pipes is sufficient for several persons at a time. The women are more fond of smoking the Kalian than men.

Another place of enjoyment and sociability is the bath-house. Among the Persians, religion or custom requires frequent ablutions. There are no conveniences in the houses for that purpose, but they have public baths, so that everyone may enjoy himself in them by paying fifteen cents for two hours' bathing. These baths are very necessary for women. They will get together once a week and go to these places, and spend sometimes a half a day in dyeing their hair, eyebrows, and eye-lashes. These houses are built under the ground, so that they may be supplied with water running through the city. They are heated with weeds, thornbushes, wood, etc. They are kept heated to such a high temperature that often persons that are not accustomed to the bath will faint the first time they try it. In the villages,

where there are no public baths, the women find a
warm place in the stables, where they take jars of
hot water and spend a few minutes in bathing and
chatting.

The other chance of social life for women is visiting. This gives good opportunity for sociability to
a woman that has been kept at home for a long time
by a cruel husband. Sometimes she will stay as long
as she wishes to and do talking some way. Perhaps
she will not have another such a chance for a long
time. Another thing, in visiting, she feels free and
fresh, because there is no one to rule over her. While
she is in her own home she is almost a slave to her
husband; because the husband has no idea of the
love that should exist between him and his wife, as
it is commanded in the Book of God, where it says
that a man should love his wife "even as Christ also
loved the church." This great word, "love," has no
influence upon the husband toward his poor wife.
The relation of a husband to his wife has hardly any
similarity to that of a Christian husband. He does
not marry a woman as a helpmeet or as a companion,
but for pleasure and the lusts of the flesh, and as a
slave; therefore he has no feeling of obligation to
love her, or to sympathize with her, or to help and
honor her as his own body. The wife never sits at
a feast table with her husband's guests, nor receives
male visitors. The latter must not even inquire
about her health or refer to her. When the husband
calls for her to perform some duty, he calls her by

nicknames, which are very amusing. When a husband eats, the wife can not sit with him and eat at the same time, or at the same table; but she must stand before him with her hands crossed on her breast, and ready to serve him while he is eating. After he is done, she will pour water on his hands; he will wash, and then she will wipe them with a towel, prepare his water-pipe and give it to him. While he is enjoying himself, she will take her small children to the corner of the room, turning her face to the black wall, so that her master can not see her lips moving. They have no consultation with each other about the home affairs at all. The husband thinks that the wife has no sense; or else he does not think that he needs her at all. When he goes on a journey, he will not say good-bye to her; and he does not care to look after her welfare. If she needs anything, he will write to his brothers or father or some one else. Nor will he trust her with anything, such as giving her money for her living expenses; but he will give the money to a friend, and ask him to give it to her little by little.

To show more forcibly the hard feeling of a husband toward his wife, we will quote the following story from Mr. Wilson's "Persian Life and Customs."

"There was a man who had a wife who was the plague of his life. At last, vexed beyond endurance, he put her in a deep well, determined to leave her to her fate. Three days afterward he repented, and let down a rope to release her. In the place of the woman, an immense dragon came out. Instead of devouring the man, it overwhelmed him with thanks and promises of favor for delivering it from such terrible company. To recompense him, the dragon entered into a plot that the woman should remain in the well; but it would wind itself around the daughter of the king, and, when no astrologer or charmer could release her, the man should come, and, at his bidding, it would leave. Then the king would give him a large reward: but one condition was laid down, that if ever the dragon wound itself around any other princess, the man should not molest it on pain of death. The plot was carried out. At the man's bidding, the dragon fled, freeing the princess, who was given in marriage to her deliverer with an abundant dowry. But soon the dragon captured a Frank princess. Then the king of Frankistan, having heard of the fame of this man, sent an embassy to Persia, requesting that he be sent to her relief. After many excuses and much delay, the man, at the king's command, departed for Frankistan, filled with fear as to what might be the result if he broke his contract with the dragon. On the way, however, he hit upon an expedient: so, having reached the presence of the Frank princess, he said to the dragon: 'I have not come to release the princess, but only to tell you that that woman has got out of the well, and is coming to attack you as quickly as possible.' The dragon had such a vivid recollection of its former experiences, that it fled in haste. It knew that it was 'better to dwell in a wilderness than with a contentious and angry woman.'"

This is very little about the condition of women in Persia. I wish I could bring more forcibly to the hearts of the Christian women the unsaved and awful condition of women in my country. I wish I could pierce every heart with the two-edged sword of love, and the Spirit of God, and Christ, who died to save all mankind. So would I arouse a godly zeal, and with it, perfect love and an interest in sending them full salvation from all sin, which comes only through faith in Jesus Christ. There is no other way to civilize those people, or any other people in all the world, so that poor woman will be freed from slavery, except by the gospel of Jesus Christ. I am not talking from my own experience, but from the influence that the gospel has had in past centuries, and has now in our day. Just let us look at the families that live next to us, those that have Christ, and those that have the devil. Soon we will see how great a difference is between them—as much difference as between the light of the day and the darkness of the night. The only hope is Christ. "I am the way, the truth, and the light." "No man cometh unto the father but by me."

All the male members of a family bring their brides to live under the parental roof; and one "lodge" may contain as many as three generations of married couples with their families. On becoming an inmate of her father-in-law's house, each

Persian woman has to learn the necessity of silence. Until she becomes the mother of three or four children, she is the family drudge, and may not speak to anyone but her husband; and not to him in the presence of his parents. She talks to her children, and to the youngest females of the household; but she can not speak freely until the birth of her fourth child. Then she takes high grade in the house, and eventually rules it, if she is left a widow.

The Persian woman is veiled out of doors. If she is unveiled, it is regarded as the sign of a bad woman. The street or out-door costume of a Persian woman consists of four simple articles. "Chadrah" is a dark blue or black sheet of cotton or silk, about two yards and a half one way, and two yards the other. This is put over the head and falls to the ankles, enveloping the whole body, and is held with the hands from the inside. The veil is of white cotton or linen, tied around the head over the dark Chadrah, covering the face, and hanging a little way down in front. Across the eyes is a narrow strip of lace work, through which the woman can see and get her breath, but no one can see her. "Yarim Jorah" (or bloomers) are a pair of loose trousers, with stockings of the same material attached to them. The stockings fit tightly on the feet, and are gathered at the ankles. The material for this garment is usually of brighter color than that of the "Chadrah."

The shoes are something like sandals, made of

sheepskin, and usually colored red or yellow. They cover the toes, but have nothing to stay them at the heels, so that at every step the heels of the shoes clatter in a musical way. These women have no need for shoe-buttoners, as they can easily slip their shoes off or on.

This is the complete street costume. When the woman is thus dressed, no one can see any part of her person. The woman sometimes tries to find opportunity to push her veil aside in order to get a fresh breath of air. This is admissible if there are no men about; but they sometimes do it for the purpose of disclosing their beauty and charms to attract the young men who may be passing by.

There is only one thing about the indoor costume that will be interesting to the reader. That is the head-dress. First comes a cap, made of shawls, or silk embroidered at the borders, with some pieces of money dangling at the front. It is put on the head so that the pieces of money will fall on the forehead. Over the cap is a large triangular kerchief. It is tied under the chin, covering the ears entirely, and one side of it furnishes what is called the "Yashmak," the mouth cover. This might be called the bridle, for it is intended to answer that purpose; and the mouth-piece must be kept in place, sometimes covering the nose also, as a sign that she is not allowed to talk under any circumstances, right or wrong. This is worn by all women. Brides are required to wear it more strictly than others. They are not allowed to speak a word aloud for years after marriage. Some of them never speak to their fathers- and mothers-in-law all their lives. This is considered the most proper way for a woman to show her respect for them and all the relatives of her husband. It is a wonder that they do not lose the voice and power of conversation altogether. They believe this is the only way to preserve peace in a house where so many live together. Persian women do not generally wear stockings in the house. They seem to prefer bare feet. This custom is prevalent all through the East. The men, as well as the women, are careful to cover their heads at all times, even at home, while little attention is paid to the covering of the feet. This is exactly contrary to the American ideas.

The Persian women are endowed with a natural beauty. They resemble greatly their fair Georgian neighbors, so famous for their beauty. Their complexion is clear, the features regular, and the eyes always black. The eyebrows are arched, black and heavy, the hair straight and black, the lips thin, and the teeth almost perfect. There is not a solitary woman in Persia with artificial teeth, or gold-filled ones.

We have shown the low state of woman in Mohammedanism. Let us pass from Mohammedanism to other faiths. The religion of India has properly been called "the religion of despair." In early ages, Hindooism smiled upon woman and protected her virtues; but this lasted only for a while. In its place a different system has been planted, which puts her in the lowest rank of society. Every hope that she has is founded on her husband; without him she is nothing and soulless, and a husband must constantly be revered as a god by a virtuous wife. When they are left widows, they are thenceforth regarded as dead while living. Buddhism teaches the inferiority and slavery of woman. In all past centuries of heathendom, woman has been accounted inferior in everything. Socrates utters: "Is there a human being with whom you talk less than with your wife?" and Aristotle talks about woman as an inferior being, etc. None of these can throw a ray of comfort on woman. Every one of them tries to crush the soul of a woman and to destroy her yearning after the divine love of God.

There is no hope for woman but in Christianity. Where Christianity arises, with it is the bloodstained banner of Jesus; and, with its glad tidings of salvation that saves from sin, it brings healing for all the woes and diseases of humanity, and free salvation to all nations, races, and sexes, and makes them equal in Jesus Christ, the crucified one. When we speak of Christianity, we do not mean a religion that teaches sinning every day of the life, and that we can not be free from sin while we are in the flesh. The writer has seen men, who possess a kind of Christianity, treat their wives nearly as badly as those that have no religion. But we mean the pure and holy, perfect and Christlike religion that is taught on every page of the Holy Book of God. Perhaps it will be profitable to the reader to refer to some of the golden sentences, concerning the equality of male and female, which were uttered by the lips of the dear Master, who died not only for men, but for women too. In saving, sanctifying, and purifying their souls and hearts, we will see him with the Samaritan woman at Jacob's well. This is mentioned in the fourth chapter of St. John, and is one of his most deeply spiritual conversations. We find him so anxious to save her precious soul that hunger is forgotten, and the intense heat of the summer sun did not have any effect on him. Again we see him on another occasion, pouring out his love and sympathy on the woman that was brought to him by the self-righteous Pharisees, that he might condemn her for adultery. The simple answer of the Savior was: "He that is without sin among you, let him first cast a stone at her"; and his own command to her, after relieving her of her persecutors, was, "Go and sin no more." The dear Master extended his hand of mercy, healed their sick, and raised their dead; and some way the women loved him and followed him unto his death, and were first at the resurrection. The last command of our Master was to, "Go and preach the gospel to all nations," without difference of races or sexes. Nothing will lift up woman to an equality with man but the religion of Christ, which takes out all prejudice toward opposite sexes and different races.

CHAPTER IX.

Village and Business Life in Persia.

The majority of the population of Persia are peasants; the remainder are farmers and gardeners. As a people they have few wants and fewer comforts. The contrast between the Persian and the American farmers is great. The American farmers are land owners, but the Persian farmers do not own the land they cultivate, and have no expectation of becoming property holders.

The farmers go long distances to their work. The plows used by them are of two kinds. One is very small, and the other is a little larger. The point of each is covered with iron. The land is generally plowed three times, and then the fields are divided into sections in order to facilitate irrigation. The seed is carried in a sack on one arm, and, after being planted, is watered with the other. There are no fences. The fields extend for miles without interruption, except by water courses with trees planted beside them. The reaper bends over his work with a short sickle in one hand, and, at times, he carries in the other a stick, nearly a foot long, fastened with bands of leather so that he may grasp a larger bundle. A Persian family, consisting of father and mother, sons and daughters, brides, bridegrooms, and grandchildren, live together in such harmony as might be expected among rival wives and different sets of children. A swinging hammock holds the youngest baby. The other children, in a state of nudity and often sore-eyed, receive very little care.

The travelers are accustomed to salute the harvesters with these words, "May God give you strength." The reply is thus, "Your coming is pleasing, may God keep you." The traveler replies, "May your harvest be blest." The harvester responds, "May your life be prolonged." The sheaves are taken to the threshing floor on wooden wagons or donkeys. Plain carts, drawn by oxen or buffalos, are sometimes used in transporting the crops. The carts are carefully constructed and are very durable. The length of the cart is twenty feet, and the bed is six feet wide at the back and gradually narrows until it reaches a point at the end of the tongue. The wheels have heavy spokes, on the ends of which are arcs of wood. Other wheels are made of solid blocks of wood, and are encircled by broad iron tires. The threshing-floors are located beside the village and are close together for safety and convenience. The ground is leveled off in plats and hardened. In the center of each plat a staple is fastened and to it a pole is attached. The oxen or horses, being tied to the pole, are made to walk over the land and thus thresh out the grain. Several kinds of threshing machines are used. One contains a roller about six feet in diameter. The roller is covered with iron teeth arranged in a circle. As the oxen draw it, it revolves, and by this method the straw is thoroughly cut up and the wheat loosened. The frame of the threshing machine is turned up at one end like a sled. A man sits upon this and drives the oxen. A wooden fork is used to cast the straw before the wind and the chaff is blown aside. The cut straw is stored away for fodder and plastering.

A peculiar crop is that of thorns. On the uncultivated land and the fields, after harvest, spring up great quantities of camel thorns. These are brought home and used for baking bread, burning lime or brick, heating bath houses, and feeding donkeys and camels. The farmer rotates his crops, and fertilizes with manure and ashes. Earth from old walls is highly valued as a fertilizer. Irrigation greatly enriches the land. Grain is sometimes stored in pits which have been plastered and lined with straw. The land owners often keep storehouses of wheat waiting for a rise in the price. Lack of snow or rain in the winter quickly raises the price.

Irrigation demands much attention from the farmer. Every river, creek, and spring is utilized. At some distance up a stream the channel is dug and the water taken off on a higher level. The water follows the crooks of the valley and goes far up into the gullies, preserving an approximate level. It distributes its supply over the low land.

The herds of cattle are pastured in common by herdsmen or boys. The watch dogs are fierce and are terrors to the stranger. Sometimes yokes are put on these dogs to prevent them from jumping over walls and trespassing in the vineyards. Flocks consist of sheep, goats, cows, buffalos, horses, donkeys, and camels. Sheep and goats are valued for their milk. From this, cheese is made. Mutton is of more value than beef.

The Persian sheep is noted for its large tail, which is a mass of fat, often forty pounds in weight. They are supported on a little wagon to prevent their dragging on the ground.

The writer has been asked time and again, "What do the people in Persia do for their living?" In the cities, the open bazaars furnish the answer. The bazaar (market) is not only a place of barter, but constitutes an extensive manufacturing establishment. Many of the shops are factories, though each one is on a small scale. There is no machinery. The greatest advance is in the use of sewing machines, treadles, and imported hand tools. All the methods of manufacture are open to the view of the passer-by. Some tradesman are seen carding wool and making *kecha* or felt matting; others are pulling cotton fiber and making quilts. In the timber bazaar, men are sawing boards with long handsaws; a little further on, carpenters are making them into doors and windows. Others are sawing out the teeth of wooden combs; the confectioner is seen pulling his taffy, and crushing rice into flour with a great sledgehammer; the restaurateur chopping meat and mixing with it garlic and onions to make *spish cahohs;* the baker is kneading dough, heating the ovens, and throwing on pegs the sweet-smelling *sangong* (kind of bread), while he talks across the fifteen foot street to the chandler who is pouring candles into moulds before the gaze of all. Scores of braziers, turners, tailors, silversmiths are busy at work, stopping only to wait on their customers. They make some goods to order, but especially prepare a stock for the surrounding towns and villages. Articles of wool, silk, and cotton goods are woven on hand looms at home. Carpets and rugs are made in the villages. Each shopkeeper is a small capitalist, and has "kronag" (apprentices), whom he feeds and clothes, and each of whom hopes soon to set up a separate shop.

The Mohammedan has an advantage over the Christian, not only because his co-religionist is willing to sell to him cheaper than to others, but because, in the case of vegetables, meat, or anything that is moist, and sometimes in the case of dry articles of food, the Christian is not allowed to touch them. For this reason there are no Christian bakers, butchers, or fruit-dealers in Persian cities.

Again, if a Mohammedan is under the business necessity of entering a Christian home, he will not drink from his cups, or even in his house unless it is made by a Mohammedan; he will not smoke a pipe after a Christian. Mohammedans have been abused and beaten for taking meals with Christians. Vessels, also, if used by a Christian, are defiled and unfit for use. A coffee vessel may be purified by immersing it in water, or by pouring water over it, or by repeating the creed over it; but an earthen vessel must be broken.

This defilement is supposed to reach foods and drinks and the vessels containing them. A street beggar, with not a clean square inch upon his body, has been known to ask alms of a Christian and then wash the money before putting it into his pocket. Of course all this comes of their religious usages. Mohammedans believe all outside of the Mohammedan faith to be infidels.

There are many classes of merchants in Persia. Suppose one starts from B, with the goods or wares of that city; he goes to C, sells what he can, and replenishes his stock with various kinds of goods that he did not have before; at C he remains awhile, trading, and finally sets off for D; there he disposes of his Persian stock and buys European goods, soon returning to make a profitable exchange in the Persian markets. The wholesale trade is confined largely to imported goods: as cotton, wool, tea, sugar, etc. Goods are sold on long time, at large risk, and therefore at high prices. The gain at retail is sometimes one hundred per cent. The duty on merchandise, according to treaty, is five per cent. The standard weight is the "miscal," one hundred of which equal one "hopta," while it takes five American pounds to equal one *hopta*, eight hopta make one *hatmon*, four hatmon one *khoncarn*. With this measure they weigh raisins, molasses, and tobacco; ten hatmons make one *choonal*, with which they weigh grain, wheat, etc.

The money is made of copper and silver, with very little gold money. The bankers sit on small rugs before their shops, with boxes of money in their laps, their chief business through the day being to change money. For changing twenty cents into coppers they charge one cent, and the fee increases in proportion to the amount of the bill changed. Such is the banking system of Persia.

Rates of interest, especially among Mohamme-dans, is very high, being from twelve to twenty per cent. per annum. In banks, stores, and government offices, and in the houses of nobility, are a class of men employed as clerks and secretaries; they are called "Mirza." The mirza is the master of the pen, and can write beautifully and correctly. His outfit consists of a Kalomdon and a roll of paper. The Kalomdon is a pen case, about eight or ten inches long and one and one half inches wide, which is carried in his girdle or pocket. It is usually made of papier-mache, ornamented with pictures of flowers and animals, or men and women of the royal family. The contents of the case are a small inkholder of brass or silver (sometimes of gold), some pens, and a pen-knife, a piece of bone, a small spoon, and a pair of scissors. The pens are stiff reeds of the same kind that were used for writing on papyrus or parchment. The pen-knife and bone are used for sharpening the pen; the point of the reed is laid upon the bone to be cut to the proper bluntness; the scissors are used for trimming the paper; the spoon is used to pour water on ink and wet it.

There is no gas nor electric lights in the streets of a Persian city. The mayor appoints an officer who has a number of assistants to watch over the city day and night. Every night of the year receives from the mayor a special name: as dog, lion, kismet, etc. These words are known only to the officials and those persons who have been commanded to be out at a late hour of the night. If an officer finds a man on the street after 9 o'clock, he calls to him to give the name of the night; should he fail to do this, he is arrested and kept all night, and if he has no good reason for being out, he is fined before he is dismissed.

Persian cities have large graveyards, some of them containing from five to ten acres of land. Mohammedans dig up the remains of dead relatives and carry them to Mecca, Medina, Korhalah, or to some other sacred place. The most picturesque of workmen is the barber, who may be frequently seen plying his trade. In all Eastern countries the barber is a much respected functionary, yet shaving is by no means the comfortable luxury in the East that it is among Western people. An Oriental barber shop in cities is usually found on some street aside from the main thoroughfare. Here the white-robed attendant waits upon his patron, seating him upon a chair or stool, or upon the floor. Tying a large towel about the neck of the sitter, the barber is ready to begin. An attendant usually holds a dish of water while the operation is in progress. The upright position is not calculated to add to the comfort of the patron, but this is atoned for, to some extent, by the skill and deftness with which the razor is handled by the barber. The operator rubs the scalp gently and comfortably for a considerable time with his fingers, moistened with water, and afterwards applies the razor, shaving from the crown downward. Some classes in the East shave the head, or at least a portion of its surface, at regular intervals, and others the face alone. Shaving the head was⋅customary among the Hebrews as an act of mourning, and was probably performed in the same manner as is now usual in those latitudes. The ancient nations attached great value to the possession of a beard. In Egypt, however, it was the common practice to shave the hair of the face and head. Herodotus mentions it as a peculiarity that they permitted the hair of the head to grow as a sign of mourning. It is supposed that, during their captivity, the Israelites preserved their beards. The Assyrians, Amalekites, Canaanites, and Arabians were all more or less bearded in early times. One of the very oldest traditions is that Adam was created with a beard. Modern Mohammedans no longer regard the beard as a sacred thing, as once did the followers of Islam.

CHATER X.

CHRIST'S COMMAND.

Our great Captain has left us His marching order: "Go ye into all the world and preach the gospel to every creature."

God, the Father, created all the world; Christ, the Son of Man, died for every creature. The color, white or black, red or yellow, has no significance in His sight. He does not despise His own works. There is no *great*, no *small*.

The nations, made of one blood in the Father's house, have disunited and retired to the several parts of the earth, having now mutual hatred and prejudice. Christ came down from the high throne to bring them together for the great reunion of His family, under the banner of the common Fatherhood of God and the common brotherhood of Man.

The spirit of the evangelization of the world, therefore, is the spirit of Christ, and is the characteristic of Christianity, which proves it to be of divine origin. David Livingstone well said, "The spirit of Missions is the spirit of our Master, the very genius of His religion. A diffusive philanthropy is Christianity itself. It requires perpetual propagation to test its genuineness." Being of divine origin, Christianity satisfies the religious nature of all human beings. It suits every creature; it is the light of the world, while Confucianism flourished only in

China, Mohammedanism in Turkey, Buddhism only twinkles in Asia, as the light of stars or moon. Buddhism or Mohammedanism, sparkling in Asiatic night, shall fade away before the "Sun of Righteousness." God, having already given the railroad and steamship to us, having taught us the sciences and arts, having digged gold and silver for us, having disclosed the mystery of Nature's power,—all things being prepared, now commands us, His disciples, to "Go and teach all nations, baptizing them in the name of the Father, and of the Son, and of the Holy Ghost."

If, "Whatsoever He saith unto you, do it," is the command, it is the duty of the loyal and loving Christians, and the faithful churches, to yield to the words of authority.

Disobedience is sin. We can not understand why there are some who profess Christianity and yet oppose foreign missions. There is no such term as "anti-foreign mission" in the vocabulary of a Christian.

Cry for Help.

"Come over into Macedonia, and help us," is the cry incessantly coming from the four winds of the earth to the churches.

This being the age of the evangelization of the world, God has prepared the hearts of the heathen world for the reception of the gospel; and, moreover, modern civilization, which they have adopted more

or less, has convinced them sufficiently of the inferiority of their religion to Christianity. The world
is now ready for the glad tidings of the "Man of
Galilee."

"Lift up your eyes and look on the fields, for they
are white already unto harvest": 400,000,000 of China,
285,000,000 of India, 250,000,000 of Africa, 20,000,-
000 of Korea, 40,000.000 of Japan, 11,000,000 of
Persia are crying for help.

Once impenetrable Africa is now opened; the
long wall of China is broken; and never was there a
riper field than India.

Persia, under the oppression of Moslem, stretches
her imploring hand toward a Christian country. The
cry is two-fold—from the Christian as well as the
heathen. The Christians cry for the reinforcement of
their churches from abroad. They are faithful, strong
soldiers, always ready to die martyrs. Christian
Armenians were crying for help, and were massacred,
not obtaining any response to their cries. The Persian Nestorians, oppressed by the intolerable Moslems,
are crying for help. The scattered Christians
throughout the heathen world, full of love and pity,
are calling for help.

The honest seekers of the light cry for help, for
the Brahma-Somaji system of philosophy, or the
theosophical society in India, or the "new religion,"
or the conglomeration of Buddhism and Unitarianism
in Japan, can not satisfy their innermost religious
nature.

The patriots, who read the history of Greece and Rome, of Egypt and China, cry for help, recognizing that Christianity is the basis of healthy civilization and the foundation of a nation's strength.

The masses cry for help, realizing that neither pessimistic Buddhism, nor fatalistic Mohammedanism can give them hope to heal their wounded hearts and cheer their broken spirits in their struggle of life. "A voice from heaven" from the "Unknown God," is the thing they are searching and crying for. They cry toward high heaven, cry to the churches, cry to the Christians.

> "The nations call from sea to sea;
>   Extend the thrilling cry;
> 'Come over, Christians, if there be,
>   And help us, ere we die.'"

The Mission.

The mission of the churches is not to take the liturgies and the creeds, but Christianity. The missionaries were not commanded to introduce a pope or a bishop, but Christ. The world does not cry for the sects or "isms," but "the Christianity of Christ."

The world, moreover, is to be taught Christ's idea of an individuality as well as His salvation. Roman Catholicism does not supply the demand. God entrusted the world's evangelization to the Protestant nations, especially to the Anglo-Saxon race, as He entrusted, in the days of old, the infusion of the

monotheistic idea to the people of Israel. Let not
the world be disappointed by your slow response to
their call. Nay, let not "the heathen" be amazed
by your "civilized" action, sending them opium
and rum, gunboats and Krupp guns, instead of the
Bible. Asia drinks more, smokes more, and has
increased the demoralizing element since the intro-
duction of the Western civilization. A Mohammedan calls the drunken man a "Christian." The
writer prays that the Japanese, who never before
learned how to chew tobacco, may never be so highly
civilized as to use it. It is stated that New York,
with a population of 5,000,000, produces more murderers than Japan with 40,000,000 souls. London is
proverbial for the amount of its pauperism, and Christendom generally for its gambling and drinking habits. Christendom has the greatest darkness with the
greatest light; for the shadow is deeper, the brighter
the light that casts it. The churches must be the
light of the world, and the salt of the earth. The
church must be the conscience of the nation. The
present churches of Christendom need the baptism
of the Holy Spirit. Yet the good fruit which we
find in Christendom is such as the combined force of
Mohammedanism, Confucianism, and Buddhism can
never bring forth. Where, in the heathen world, can
we find a Washington, a Howard, a Wilberforce, a
Gladstone, a Florence Nightingale, or a Frances
Willard? Mr. K. Uchimura, the author of " How I
Became a Christian," said: "Gentleman,—I doubt

whether such is possible, without the religion of Jesus Christ to mould us. The Christian, the God Almighty's gentleman,—he is a unique figure in the world, indescribably beautiful, noble, and lovable." The heathen needs Christianity, and even a civilized heathen needs it. God commanded the churches to send it. I said above that the Anglo-Saxon has the mission to spread the gospel of our Master. He gave them the inexhaustible wealth of India, Australia, and North America; He gave them the territories and provinces throughout the wide world, so that they may mingle with other peoples; He gave them the highest type of civilization; He disclosed to them the inalienable right of man — liberty and equality; He taught them the worth of woman; He revealed to them the mystery of the Scriptures — these advantages He bestowed upon them that He may use them as the instruments for the Christianization of the whole world. The heathen knows already the fruit of heathenism, and will let the Christians show the beauty of their religion. They are crying for light and life.

The nineteenth century is closing, and the dawn of a new century soon will break upon us. Let the close of this century be characterized by the great movement of the world's evangelization. The church was divinely instituted to disseminate the truth. The invincible army of Christ, under the banner of the cross, starting from Jerusalem, conquered the Romans and the Teutons, and, crossing the Atlantic, landed

on the American continent. Now, crossing the
Pacific, it has reached Japan; it is marching through
Corea, China, India, and Africa, and will soon go
back to its own home victorious — the dawn of the
millennium. The coming of this golden millennium
greatly depends upon the attitude of the churches of
Christendom. Let the hands respond to the lips that
send up the prayer, "Thy Kingdom come." Let the
men and women who sing,

> "From Greenland's icy mountains,
>   From India's coral strand,
>   Where Afric's sunny fountains
>   Roll down their golden sand,
> From many an ancient river,
>   From many a palmy plain,
> They call us to deliver
>   Their land from error's chain,"

respond to this call.

When the voice of the Lord is heard, "Whom
shall I send, who will go for us?" who can answer,
"Here am I, send me?" The mission work is two-
fold — *send* or *go*. "Go," is the command of the
Lord; "Come and help us," is the cry of the world,
and the duty of the church is to send.

The Missionary.

The missionary must be well equipped, both spirit-
ually and intellectually.

All the heathen are not those who live in the
jungles of Africa. The missionaries must combat
materialism, agnosticism, rationalism, and higher

criticism (which are, to a certain extent, ruling the heathen minds already), besides the religions in their countries. As Paul, the greatest of the apostles, was a missionary to the Gentile world, so the present missionaries to the foreign fields must be men and women worthy of the name, "Ambassadors of Christ."

They ought to come to fulfill the *ideal* of their religion, and not to destroy, for such was the spirit of Christ. The best converts of the heathen are those who keep the beauties of their religions, for every heathen religion has its own characteristic beauty.

The missionaries ought to be very careful not to hurt the sentiment of the people by misrepresenting the country.

The missionary spirit must have been originated by the spirit of love, instead of pity, considering them as the brothers and the sisters, and not as "the poor heathen," or "the inferior race."

Conclusion.

The writer believes that the most effective and economical way of the evangelization of a heathen country is to give the youth of that country a Christian education, and use them as the instruments for its Christianization. As the writer, Bro. Basil Sarmast, Persian, who was educated in his country, and completed his Biblical study in the United States of

America, now returns to his mother's home to see his loved ones again, to tell them the sweet story of the cross, he most humbly prays the Almighty Hand will use him for the conversion of that land. "God be with you till we meet again at Jesus' feet."

CHAPTER XI.

PERSIA NEEDS THE GOSPEL.

The question has been asked time and again, "Is there any missionary in Persia?" Before showing the need of the gospel, it will be better to give a short history of Missions in Persia. Missions were begun in Persia in the sixteenth century by Roman Catholic workers, and they made an effort among the Nestorians in the eighteenth century, which was very successful. Large missions of French Lazarists and nuns were established in 1841. There are from ten to fifteen thousand Roman Catholics in Persia. But I am glad to say that they are losing ground instead of gaining. The first Protestant missionaries were Moravians, who, in 1747, came to preach the glad tidings of salvation. Owing to some disturbed conditions, however, they did not remain long.

In 1811 Henry Martyn visited Persia. He was one of God's noblemen of this century, and traveled through Persia declaring the truths of the gospel among fanatical Mohammedans. He left as a memorable testimony of his love, the translation of the New Testament, and probably the Psalms, into the Persian language. Some efforts were made to reach the Jews and Mohammedans through the work of the missionaries of the London Society, also through Basilian missionary societies, but their labors were afterward abandoned. The first Protestant mission

was established in 1835 by Revs. J. Parkins and
A. Grant, M. D., in Oroomiah, by the American
Board. It was called the Mission of the Nestorians.
The founders of this mission were godly men and
women; but it is to be regretted that their successors
became very cold and almost lost the spirit of aggress-
iveness possessed by the founders.

In 1856 they had one hundred and fifty-six communicants; in 1870 they numbered 763. In 1870
Teheran (the capital) was occupied, and Tohrig in
1873. Altogether they (American Presbyterians,
"Old School") have five stations. During sixty-three
years they report two thousand seven hundred and
sixteen communicants from Armenian and Nestorian
Christians. Of this we will give an account later on.

First.—Persia Needs Christianity.

The universal religion is Mohammedanism, whose
chief watchword from the past until the present has
been, "The sword is the key of heaven and of hell;"
meaning that those who accept Mohammedanism,
even from the terrors of the sword, shall be
saved, while those who reject it shall die and be
damned. When the priest or mujtahid goes to the
mosque, sometimes he carries a wooden sword in one
hand and the Koran in the other, to fulfil the command of the great prophet, who said, the conquest
of the Koran over Judaism or Christianity is to be
accomplished by the sword. From that time till
now, it has been taught to the people that their wars

are holy wars, and that the Mohammedan soldier is
the executor of God's will and vengeance. No military service is required of either Jews or Christians,
as they can not be depended upon to defend Mohammedanism. But while they are free from military
service, frequently they have to pay a certain amount
of money for the support of the army and state.

The sad experience of thirteen hundred years
has shown that neither obedience nor submission can
secure to us the safety of our mothers, sisters, wives,
and property. These long years we have submitted
to the fanatical Mohammedans, and have been suffering persecutions. We say that we need Christianity,
not only for our own sakes, but for the sake of the
souls of our persecutors. As has been mentioned, Mohammedanism came and brought the sword and bloodshed; but Christianity came and brought peace, good
will, and good feeling toward men (Luke 2:14). Mahomet brought damnation to the soul, but Christ
brought "Holiness and righteousness" (Luke 1:75).
There is no happiness, joy, and safety in this universe
to the human soul, outside of Christianity. If I say
that Persia needs Christianity, I mean what I say.
Pray for Persia.

*Second.—Persia Needs the Gospel to Protect Our
Women.*

As has been indicated before, Mohammedanism
teaches, or rather allows, all its believers to marry
four legal wives and slave women without number;

and there are three other kinds of marriage, concu-binage, exchange marriage, and temporary marriage. The latter is when a man is on a journey. Marriage is one of the principal doctrines of the Koran. Many beautiful girls and women have been converted by force to the faith of the Moslems. Girls have often been stolen when alone in the fields and vineyards. Mothers fear for their daughters, and advise them not to wash their faces nor put on nice clothes, lest a Mohammedan would be attracted by their beauty. A Mohammedan believes that God created all beautiful girls for the followers of Mahomet. When a girl is converted by force to Mohammedanism, there is no use of complaining to the government, as the gov-ernment is Mohammedan. It is the Mohammedan doctrine that when a man converts a Christian, he has done a good thing, and all his sins will be forgiven.

In 1891 a band of mounted Kurds came one night to a village about fifty miles from where the writer lives, where a Christian family was residing and carried off a beautiful girl, compelling her to become a Mohammedan and to marry the son of a Kurdish sheik (priest). The family were British subjects. The acting British consul demanded that the girl be released and returned to her mother. The Kurds answered that the conversion to Islam was of the girl's own free will. The consul demanded that the girl should be brought before a proper tribunal to answer for herself. This the Kurds refused. Other efforts were made to release the girl, but without result, except the killing of several of the Persian soldiers. Finally the Kurds yielded and brought the girl to the Persian authorities, after her purity was taken from her. At a formal examination before the officials, the consul, and her mother, the girl stated that she had of her own will married the Kurd and become a Mohammedan. This is not the only one that has been made a Mohammedan thus; but hundreds of our pure girls have been wrecked in the past. This robbery still continues. It is the same way with a married woman, if she is beautiful. But if Christianity takes hold of the people in Persia, they will affirm, not what is taught in the Koran by Mahomet, that gives them freedom to do what they please with people that are outside of their own faith, but will affirm the tenth commandment, "Thou shalt not covet thy neighbor's house, nor his wife, nor anything that is thy neighbor's." They will follow Christ's teaching, who said, "That whosoever looketh on a woman to lust after her hath committed adultery with her already in his heart." There is no such a command or teaching in any creed of the different faiths in the world, except in the Christian's creed. The cry comes from all the unchristianized parts of the world, "Come and save us from the corruption of body, soul, and spirit." Why is it that a man is held superior to a woman, not only in Persia, but in all heathendom? We read in the Word of God, "God made them male and female, and gave them dominion." We do not find in any place in the Book of

God anything concerning the inequality of the sexes. But the standard of Christianity shows the woman has some rights over man, as man has over the woman. The writer believes that man must have more love toward woman than the woman toward the man, especially those men that are sanctified; as much as we enjoy our experience of sanctification, so much we have to love our wives. Dr. B. Carradine, in one of his books, calls woman the "second blessing." I was prejudiced myself on that line, that man ought to have superiority over woman; but, thank God, for a little more than two years (1898) since God sanctified my soul under the preaching of a godly woman (Mrs. Mary McGee Hall) I have been made free from sin; not only that, but from everything that is contrary to the will of God. To-day Christianity opens its joyful gates and takes in all the women of the world, as well as the men. It gives glad tidings of peace and hope for this life, as well as for the life to come, and presents to the world the love and power of the Son of God. He died to save from all sin anyone that comes to him, and to make them holy in this life and ready for heaven. And as the result of the teaching of the gospel of Christ, Christianity boasts of her redeemed women, whose moral, intellectual, and spiritual beauty is more attractive than any beauty of face. Again, Christianity can boast of her hundreds of thousands of women workers, that are fighting against sin, and to raise their fallen

sisters. Some of them may be mentioned here: Miss
Frances E. Willard, whose work will last till Jesus
Christ comes; Lady Henry Somerset, of England.
and Lady Ramabi, the great worker in India; Amanda
Smith, the African evangelist of holiness, Clara Barton, and hundreds of others. Nothing good, outside
of Christianity, can be accomplished. Christianity
is the only hope for fallen humanity.

Third.—Persia Needs the Gospel of Temperance.

Those who are called Mohammedans are the
strongest on Temperance. All the followers of Mahomet are commanded not to drink, not to touch, not
to taste intoxicants. They are forbidden to salute
anyone who drinks intoxicating liquor. It is written
in the Koran, they ought not to eat on the same table
with those that drink liquor. Ali (the son-in-law of
Mahomet) was asked how far we must keep from
wine. The answer was: "If a drop of wine fall into
a well of water, then let this well be filled with dirt.
After a hundred years are passed, and grass grows on
the top of that well, if a sheep comes and eats that
grass, and then that sheep goes through a flock of
sheep, you are not allowed to eat the flesh of that
flock. Again, if there is a chain of camels, one end
in the east and the other end in the west, if the burden of the last camel is wine, you are not allowed to
touch the bridle of the first one." This shows how
much hard feeling they have toward intoxicating

liquor. If we say that the Bible does not teach its
followers to be strict against intoxicating liquors, we
are mistaken. It does teach it, but I am sorry to say
that some who know the teaching of the Bible are
blinded by the devil.

There are no saloons in Persia, as far as I know,
but the Assyrians, or so-called Christians, are a great
nation for drinking wine. Many of them own great
vineyards and make from the fruit as much wine and
whisky as they wish. Wine takes the place of water,
tea, and coffee. Grapes are very cheap. The poor
man can be supplied with wine very easily. While
the people work very hard during the summer until
the last of October, nearly every kind of business is
suspended for the winter. The most of their days
are devoted to having a good time in the fatal
pleasures of the cup. They think there is no love
nor good fellowship without wine. It is that way
with many other nations of the earth to-day. When
a man has a visitor, or guest, from a distance, he will
invite all his neighbors in, so that the entire day will
be spent in eating and drinking. The next day one
of the neighbors will entertain the whole crowd, and
so on, the feast lasting for several days or weeks.
Often before the end of these days some of their number will meet death. The women are required to let
wine alone, that they may cook food for these de-
graded Christian husbands. The missionaries (Old
School Presbyterian) have said very little about it.
While they forbid their communicants using intoxi-

cants, they are not very strict concerning it. The
Missionary Report gives 2,716 communicants. I
don't think that I am mistaken in saying that fifty per
cent. of them keep intoxicating liquor in their houses.
No one can be a good temperance man or woman
if he believes in a sinning religion. There is no way
to avoid the liquor traffic and take it from the face
of the earth but through the influence of Christianity. It is the business of the true followers of Christ,
in America, to vote against the liquor traffic. Pray
God to open the eyes of the professors of religion
and all its possessors to live a sinless life; then they
can not help being temperate.

Fourth.—Persia Needs the Gospel for Temporal Improvement.

The houses are built of one story, with flat roofs,
which are very comfortable to the natives. During
hot summer nights they sleep on the housetops. In
the last ten or fifteen years people are building modern houses. The houses are very poorly kept, and
half furnished. Some of the families are large,
numbering from ten to twenty-five or thirty-five in
one house. When one marries, it is required of him
to live with his parents, and raise a family, for some
time at least. The father and mother have supreme
authority over the home. When the family gets
large, many times quarreling is heard, and sometimes
fighting. The custom demands that the son bring
his bride to the house of his father; if he does not,

he is called a prodigal. When the writer married, his wedding ceremony took place at his father's house. Some of these houses, in which very large families live, are divided into rooms. In some of these rooms there are three or four beds.

There are no railroads. A large part of the people travel by walking, while others travel on camels, donkeys, horses, and mules. A large per cent. of the people travel barefoot during warm weather. If any one uses shoes during that time, he uses no stockings. Some of them go without stockings all the year round. Very few women wear stockings at home in winter, but away from home they do. At home, they wear neither shoes nor stockings. While in America, on entering a house you have to take off your hat, in Oriental countries you have to take off your shoes and keep on your hat. Here, the knife and fork are used for eating; there, the fingers are used.

Instead of using from five to ten dishes in preparing a meal for one man there, sometimes one large dish is used for four or six men. The table on which they eat is from three to five inches high. Of course there are no chairs. The floor takes the place of chairs. They are ignorant of fashion. Many men and women do not change their clothing twice a year hardly, and often do not bathe the whole winter. As to washing of face and hands and combing of hair, they are not much in favor of it.

A large per cent. of the deaths occur in infancy. The mothers do not understand how to take care of

the children and to nourish the delicate life during
that period. The infants are not dressed warm in
many instances. Ignorantly, they expose them to
contagious disease. There are several other things
about them not to be mentioned here. Why is it
that this people are so much lower than the people
who live in America or other countries? They have
no lack of mental powers. But, while "God is no
respector of persons," there can be little improvement on any line without the Bible. What improvement is made must be through some other providen-
tial power, and will be very slow. Everywhere the
gospel goes, God sends His blessing with it. He not
only blesses the people, but the country and everything that is in it. I know from my own experience;
when I look back, I can see the great changes which
have taken place in the last fourteen years of my
life. They have come to me through the blessed
gospel, which is called the "Power of God." No one can
feel that the gospel is the "Power of God" until he becomes the child of God. Therefore, God, who reveals
himself in that gospel, is able to change not only the
spiritual state of humanity, but also the physical and
temporal conditions, too. Isaiah 1:16-19. How can
they know that is true, unless some one take to them
this blessed Book of God? Romans 10:14-16.

Fifth.—Persia Needs Religious Education.

There are many schools in the cities and in some
of the villages. These schools are in the mosques

(churches). The mollah (priest) is the teacher. Persian and Arabic are taught. The Koran is read, oftener with the eye than with the understanding. Some familiarity with the Persian poets is required. There is only one college in the whole country. That was founded by the Shah after his visit to some of the universities of Europe. Several languages are taught in that school. This college is only for princes and wealthy people. It is only one shining star in the midnight darkness. Another school was started at Oroomiah in 1836 by missionaries. The founders were men of God and full of the Holy Ghost. The school was based on the principle of spreading the gospel, which is still the purpose of the institution. But in spiritual power it is far below the work of thirty years ago. Some one may ask, Why is it so? It has been stated before, that the founders of it were full of the Spirit of God, but their successors are not so filled. This is the only school for from three to five millions of population to depend upon. This is the school from which the writer is a graduate (1890). This is one of the places which he loves greatly and for which he prays much. In such a condition this school accomplishes some good. There would be more good accomplished if this college were run on the full-salvation principles. That is what we Orientals need. Pray that God will first give full salvation to the leader of that school; then to those who come to school, and through them to the vast multitudes that are in the bondage of sin and on their way to hell. I can say freely, the school that teaches a full salvation can accomplish more in a short time than other schools can do in centuries. Asbury College, Wilmore, Kentucky, has for eight years been teaching sanctification through the baptism with the Holy Ghost. It has accomplished more good in the salvation of souls and the cause of Christ than many other schools combined that teach a sinning religion. As a native of Persia, I beg you, if you send missionaries to that country, send full salvation men and women, who will organize schools for the teaching of the Bible, out of a fully saved heart.

It is very hard to find one in ten thousand in Persia that can read and write. It is necessary in some parts of the country to walk from ten to twenty miles to find a man who can write a letter for another, while those among the females who can read are very rare. They have the desire for education, and would gladly crowd the schools. The people of the present age are hungry after everything that will do them good. One of the best ways of converting heathendom is to establish schools and bring the little ones into them and teach them the love of God. Let them be rooted and grounded in this perfect love; then send them out into different communities and the result will be seen very soon. To Christianize this lost world of ours, we need truly religious men and women and religious schools. It will take from fifty to sevent-five dollars to run a winter school in these

countries. Read Matt. 28:16-20. There are hundreds
of children that have no place to go, but run all over
town in warm and cold weather; and their parents
will be perfectly willing to send their children to
school, not only for the sake of learning, but to be
kept in where they will be free from exposure to the
weather or from accident. I believe it is in all other
countries the same as it is in Persia. There are no
places where the people will not be glad to have
schools in which their children can be taught, not
only reading and writing, but also the religion of Jesus
Christ. The only hope for the lost world is to get
the little ones to Christ. If we do not see the result
of our work in this generation, it will come out with
great force the next generation. The real source of
the power of the Roman Catholic Church is the religious training of the children. If all evangelical
churches would take an interest in getting the children saved, they would win the world much sooner
than in any other way.

Sixth.—*Persia Needs Gospel Preachers.*

The vast, glorious harvest is fully ripe, and fast
falling into the ground. The cry comes from every
quarter, "Come and help us." Now is emphatically
the most reasonable day of salvation for the thousands who are ready to receive the Bread of Life to
feed their hungry souls. There are at least two hundred thousand Nestorians to whose minds and hearts
the true gospel preacher will have as ready access as

to almost any equal population in America or any other Christianized country. The hostile character and unsettled condition of the savage Kurds may hedge up the way of the workers for a time among the Nestorians, as they are doing at the present time, but they will come sooner or later, if they see and feel the influence of the workers of the gospel. There is a great deal of difference between the present and ten years ago. The writer has traveled among them. Those who are called Nestorians are perfectly ready to accept the true religion of Jesus. What they need is only reformation. Not only are the Nestorians ready to receive the truth, but nine millions of Mohammedans also are ready. Of course the Koran forbids Christians to preach to Moslems, Some years ago no Christian dared to discuss the question of the religion of Jesus Christ with Mohammedans, or attempt to show Christ's superiority over Mahomet. If a Moslem had said to a Christian, "Mahomet was greater than Christ, and ours is the true religion; you are gavoor" (infidel), the Christian's reply was, "Yes, sir; you are right." While in some places it is so now, yet the general answer of the present day will be, "No, sir." If a Christian sees the truth clearly and knows it, his duty is to uphold it. There is now freedom of religious discussion and conversation between a Christian and a Moslem. They sometimes call at the homes of one another and talk about religion. The Christians read the Bible to them. The true

child of God feels it his duty to disclose to anyone
with whom he comes in contact the light and love
which he has in his own soul and which everyone
needs. "The harvest is great, but the laborers are
few."

Now some one may ask, "What kind of missionaries do the heathen need?"

Before answering this question, I must express my
deep gratitude and thankfulness to the missionaries of
the "Old School Presbyterian Church," because I
was trained by them and graduated in their college.
But, as a possessor of the perfect love of God, I have
to answer this according to the will of God and to
glorify His name. Since the writer gave his heart
to God he does not remember that he has ever closed
his secret prayer without asking God's blessing upon
all missionaries in the world that are working for the
salvation of souls. Not long ago I was in a camp-
meeting. There was a young lady present who was
going as a missionary to teach the children. During
one morning service, the proposition was put before
the audience, "If any one has salvation, stand up."
All Christians stood. While I was standing, I looked
around and saw that young lady sitting in her seat.
The preacher asked her if she was a Christian. The
answer was, "No." God gave me a chance that
afternoon in a missionary society. That lady was
there. Of course I did not give her name; but I
said what God had me to say. Can a sinner convert
a sinner? All heathen are sinners. So we don't

need sinner missionaries. We need missionaries that will be one with us, or a little higher. A missionary has a right to have from two to four servants. There are many that keep at least three female servants and one or two male servants, and keep two or three horses. "Well," you will say, "the missionaries have to live different from the natives." I admit that; but not live so high that the natives will be low in their eyes, as the white people look upon negroes in some parts of America. Perhaps you will say, "I do not believe what you say." If you do not, nothing I say will effect you. "They can not live," you say. Yes, they can. Are they much better than holy, sanctified Paul? Read and see what he said, as the first missionary of the Gentiles (I Cor. 9:19-26). While you read this passage, offer an earnest prayer to God to sanctify your soul, then you can say, "Yes, Lord, I will live like the natives, to win their precious souls from hell."

If the great missionary, St. Paul, were overseer of all foreign missionaries of the present time, I believe he would turn out of the work a large number of them; not because they are not very well educated, but because they have not perfect love toward a lost humanity. Nowhere does the Bible teach that we must love ourselves more than our fellowmen, but it teaches us to love our neighbor as ourselves. The Son of God did not put any difference between different classes of people, but preached to all kinds and staid with all kinds — the sinful as well as the righteous. Every one of His followers must have His spirit in their hearts. If we have the spirit of our Master, we must have the spirit of humility; if we have the spirit of humility in us, then we will have no pride. I have heard some of the children of God sing the song, "I want to be like Jesus in my heart." That is what every one of the workers in the vineyard of Christ needs.

Dear reader, I will give another fact that I read in a book that was written by a missionary. He says about all the people of that country, "Truth telling is a lost art." "People lie as long as they can find lies to tell, after which they may from accident or necessity once or twice speak the truth." Do you suppose that true? Let us not think that it is a fact. If those people were truthful people and perfect in all manner of life, they would have no need of a missionary to stay there or to go there; but you go to make them better. If they are false, to make them true. Under that statement comes the head of that country, the king. If he gets to see that book, he will not let any missionary stay there or go there. Of course that will not displease the people at all, but maybe will be an injury to the cause of the gospel. I wonder if that missionary said that thing while preaching to those people. I hope he has got the spirit of Christ in him, so that if he wants to write another book he will not write anything before praying and thinking about it. I am not writing this to offend those that are spending their money and prayers to convert the heathen. I am writing what I have seen. I am one of the missionary converts myself. I pray that God may fill your hearts with more love toward the heathen. While I am writing, I am praying that God will help me not to write anything that will injure the cause of Christ. While you are spending your money to send the gospel to heathen lands, all your work without prayer is nothing. But pray more for the missionaries. God will answer the prayer of His children and will bless the workers and their work in the foreign field.

Again, we need missionaries that will preach the Gospel of Holiness. That is to say, a religion that keeps us from sin. If a missionary should come and preach to me and urge me to be a Christian, and I should ask him, "Can I be free from sin, and not sin every day of my life?" and he should say, "No, you can not be free from sin while you are in this body of flesh, but by the grace of God you will get to heaven," we don't need such a missionary. Maybe you will say, No missionary will say that. Of course he will, because he himself don't believe in living without sin in this life. Not many years ago a man was baptized with the Spirit of God, sanctified wholly, and began to preach in his own church, where he was pastor, and then began to preach to outside people. He organized a band of young men. In a short time a missionary and some native preachers raised persecutions against them. The names of some of them were taken from the church book.

They were thought to be heretics, and were not
allowed to say or do anything in the churches, simply
because they had borne witness to the truth. They
testified that Christ is able to save from all sin, and
to keep from sin, too. The founder of Persian mis-
mions was inspired by the Spirit of God, like John
Wesley; but he was soon cut off from earth. The
missionaries, instead of encouraging their fire-baptized young men, encouraged the preachers to try to
keep them down. They do not give them a chance in
churches to speak or pray. If God commands us to
be holy and live holy and preach holiness, you have
no right to claim to be a child of God and preach a
sinning religion. If we can not be free from sin, let us
alone. Do not come and preach for us. If I sin one
sin a day, I will go to hell as certainly as if I sin a
hundred times a day. Read I John 3:8-11 and 4:17-
18. Can a man have the perfect love of God and
claim to be a child of God and keep sinning? Maybe
you will say, "No, our missionaries teach the perfect
religion, or, as it is called, sanctification." That is
impossible. How can a man preach anything that he
himself does not experience. Not long ago, one of
the best missionaries in China was sanctified by the
Holy Ghost and began to preach it. His church
called him back and, after a long trial, he was expelled
from church work. We are called to preach the truth
and full salvation to every one that comes to Him.
Nothing, at the same time and place, can both be and
not be. A man can not be both honest and dishonest

at the same time; neither can a man be both dead
and alive, a sinner and a Christian at the same time.
I wonder how an intelligent and educated man can
stand up and announce from his pulpit that the Holy
Book of God does not teach a sinless religion, or the
second work of grace, subsequent to regeneration.
If I say we heathens need a holiness missionary, I
mean one that will preach the gospel in all its fulness.
We are tired of sin and of a sinning religion. The
writer lived eleven years a converted life. During
this time he felt the need of something more, but did
not know what that something was. Thanks be to
God that filled his need a little more than two years
ago. When Christ took "the old man" out of his heart,
then he was satisfied. Read Heb. 12:14. For three
reasons everybody must get sanctified: First, this is
the will of God, the sanctification of every soul;
secondly, if we are sanctified we will work fully for
the salvation of others; thirdly, we will be willing to
endure persecutions. Maybe it will help the reader
to have just two examples of persons in whom the
love of God was perfected. In due time they gave
their lives for the sake of their Master, Jesus Christ.
The writer was acquainted with both of them; one of
them a personal friend. One of them is the case of
Mirza Abraham. He was converted through a native
preacher from the Mohammedan faith and was baptized at Khoi, his home city, and was driven out by
his family. He was arrested in Oroomiah, while telling others of his new faith and full salvation through

Jesus Christ. When brought before the governor,
he boldly testified to Christ, the Son of God and
Savior of all humanity, and to the power of the gospel. He was beaten and imprisoned. He was offered
a large amount of money if he would forsake his new
faith. Finally, he was taken to Tohrig under guard
and imprisoned. His appeals to the Shah (king)
were in vain. After suffering for almost a year, he
was choked to death by his fellow-prisoners with the
connivance of the authorities. A number of criminals, one after another, took him by the throat and
tried to make him deny Christ. He answered, "No,
Jesus is true, Jesus is true, though you slay me." He
went to heaven from prison. Their law is that the fer-
vent shall be put to death. The other was a wholly
consecrated young man, a native of Oroomiah, an Armenian, who was converted to the religion of Jesus
Christ and had Christ with all his fulness in his heart.
He was a merchant in Oroomiah, named Agajan Khan,
with a rank among the nobility, and was married
to one of a Georgian family in the Shah's service,
whose chief representative man is Persian minister
to France. (The writer saw his residence in Paris
five years ago.) His store was frequntly the place of
discussions, especially among Mohammedans; and
because of this he was hated by the mollas (priests).
His apparent prosperity also excited envy. His
enemies determined to accomplish his destruction
and laid a plot to effect this. One morning, just
before noon, a Mohammedan woman entered his

store, where some men also were present. She had been to trade with him about the sale of a certain piece of land on which he had advanced a small sum. They failed to strike a bargain, and she left the store. A Sayid rapidly spread the report that she had gone there for evil purposes. This report was given in the mosque (church) and an attack was ordered immediately. An infuriated rabble of Sayids and mollas rushed upon Agajan, threw him out into the street, kicked and beat him and dragged him through the streets. He was taken to the mosque. The chief molla, fearing he would be killed, put him in a place of refuge and fastened the door. He then said to him, "You are charged with adultery with a Mohammedan woman. Whether true or false, you can save yourself by turning Mohammedan." He refused, and promised the molla five hundred dollars if he would save him. The molla said, "No, say the creed, or they will kill you." Agajan fell on his knees for a moment of prayer, while the mob, which now filled all the courts and roofs and adjoining streets, were raging in fury for his blood. Finally they broke down the door and dragged him out, again offering him his life if he would deny his faith. They thrust him through with thirty dagger wounds and cursed his religion. At the same time he was praying to God. A rope was tied around his neck, and his body naked and beaten beyond recognition was dragged through the streets and flung into a cesspool and a dead dog thrown in beside him. There is perfect

love manifested in the lives of these two holy children of God. Can a man that is not free from sin
do this? It is impossible. May God help us to get
Christ with his fulness in our hearts and get wholly
sanctified, and then go fight the devil and all his
forces. The example of these two men, that were
killed for the sake of the Master, brought religious
freedom to the whole country.

The present Shah is a man who has a great desire
to rule in peace. He tolerates all religious beliefs,
even though they differ from his own. He is loved
by all classes of people and all religious sects, because
he is kind and considerate toward them. He is very
friendly towards the Christians. A few years ago he
visited the Presbyterian College and Ladies' Seminary and listened to some of the recitations. As an
evidence of his friendliness he was a guest at the
home of Dr. Cochran and dined with him. The
Shah has also visited a Nestorian Bishop, who resides
in a cottage so humble that some lords would be
ashamed to enter it. Of late years the royal family
has been kind to Christians. The door is open to all
Christian workers that will preach a Christ that saves
from all sin.

Seventh.—*Persia Needs the Gospel of Universal Salvation.*

The prevailing religion of Persia is Mohammedan.
In regard to the doctrine of predestination, the
Koran teaches that whatever comes, including sick-

ness, must be accepted and submitted to, without any human interference, as predestined by God from eternity. The most radical form not only leads to fatalism, but is in effect the same. This doctrine has been taught for thirteen centuries. Persia, after being under the depressing influence of the Koran for so many centuries, received the gospel in 1835. Some of the people were very glad. The gospel that was brought in 1835, in a short time became something like the Koran. The Koran does not offer universal salvation, likewise the so-called gospel given to Persia has taught for more than sixty years as follows—Confession of Faith:

1. "God from all eternity did, by the most wise and holy counsel of his own will, freely and unchangeably ordain whatsoever comes to pass.

2. "By the decree of God, for the manifestation of his glory, some men and angels are predestinated unto everlasting life, others foreordained to everlasting death.

3. "These that are predestinated and foreordained are particularly and unchangeably designed; their number is so certain that it can not be either increased or diminished. [Of course this proves that these persons thus unchangeably designed can not perish, do what they may, but will be irresistibly drawn to Christ and to justification, adoption, and sanctification.]

4. "That for these, and these only, God provided a Savior before the foundation of the world and all

means necessary to procure their salvation; which leaves no condition on their part.

5. "The rest of mankind, God was pleased according to the unsearchable counsel of his own will, whose names and numbers are also unchangeable and definitely fixed, where he extendeth or withholdeth mercy as he pleaseth, for the glory of his sovereign power over his creatures, to pass by and ordain them to dishonor and wrath and everlasting death and destruction, to the praise of his glorious justice."

From this we can learn that for these he never did provide a Savior, and that consequently they could not be saved, do what they might. We understand the above to teach, that a certain definite number of the human race are elected, unconditionally and unalterably, without reference to anything in them or to be performed by them, and of the mere good pleasure of God unto everlasting life, so that they can not perish; that the rest are so predestinated to eternal damnation, that they can not be saved, no Savior ever having been provided for them. Such is the doctrine of predestination with respect to election and reprobation of men, as held by the church that brought the gospel to Persia (Old School Presbyterians). If the gospel of Christ teaches the same thing that the Koran teaches, it is no use of trying to spread it through the country. If the gospel teaches what has been said above, the gospel is no better book than a book written by Bob Ingersoll.

According to the theory of predestination, God becomes the author of sin and injustice. The advocates of that doctrine will deny and say, "No, we don't do this in foreign fields." The writer was reared in that church, has been taught in their school, and has heard them preach, too. If anyone does not believe and accept what they teach, he will be expelled from the church. Maybe some one will ask if any one has been expelled on that line. I will say, No, because this doctrine exactly suits them. They will do as they please; at last they will go to heaven or hell. Poor, ignorant people. The writer was fourteen years of age, and newly converted. He had a discussion with an experienced preacher (I think he had fifty years' experience). For about four hours he tried to make me believe that the Bible teaches the doctrine of predestination. Thanks be to God that I had sense enough to believe that the Bible does not teach such a thing. According to the Calvinistic theory of the plan of salvation there is no use to preach at all; and there is no benefit in the death of Christ to this lost world, for the death of Christ can not bring a reprobate sinner to be saved. The confession teaches: "God from all eternity ordained whatsoever comes to pass." But man's fall came to pass, therefore God, from all eternity, did ordain man's fall. "The decree of God is the necessity of a thing" (Calvin). But man's fall is something, therefore God's decree is the necessity, or necessitating cause of man's fall. Any one who holds the theory above mentioned, can not help but make God Almighty the author of sin and all other evil things. I am not debating the question, but I am writing what I have seen and read and studied in the books that have been written by the great writers of Calvinism.

As a foreigner and lover of the Christ, I beg you not to send any one who will not teach a Savior for all, and teach that Jesus Christ died for every lost and ruined sinner. He will save every one that comes to him. "God is no respecter of persons." God loved *the world*, not a part of the world, but the whole world.

Heathendom needs the gospel that teaches a clear-cut conversion, and the doctrine of the pardoning grace of God through justification, and the renewing of our inner man by putting new life in us (regeneration), and the taking out of us of the inbred corruption, and the filling with the Holy Ghost, bringing perfect love (sanctification). This is the teaching of God's Word. But this glorious doctrine was nearly lost, when God raised up John Wesley to bring out this blessed experience of "Entire Sanctification," without which no one shall see the Lord. Not only Persians, but the whole race needs the Bible as it was taught by Christ himself and by his disciples, by James Arminius and Wesley. Do not teach the doctrine that was first held by Augustine and affirmed by John Calvin, which makes God the author of sin and every other evil. As far as I can see, the only hope for the lost humanity is through the Methodist Church and the other societies that are teaching the Wesleyan doctrine of Entire Sanctification. In any place that gospel is not preached in its fulness, there can not be improvement or progress. We need a universal, not a partial religion, and one that saves from all sin.

The writer found this full salvation from all sins, actual and inbred, January 8, 1896, in Wilmore, Ky., under the preaching of Mrs. Mary McGee Hall. I have been telling it since that time and expect to preach it till the last hours of my life.

In conclusion, the writer, a native of Persia, wishes to express his gratitude to the American Board that started mission work in Persia, to the Presbyterian Church, which, in 1871, assumed the responsibility of the work. What I said about the doctrine of that church is not from hatred or unkind feeling toward them, but, as a servant of God and washed in the blood of the Lamb, my duty is to glorify God, not man. I pray God, with his own tender mercy, to save and sanctify every one of the missionaries that are in Persia. May God open the hearts of Methodists to send Wesleyan full salvation preachers to the beloved country of mine. Dear reader, pray and help in spreading the full salvation gospel over that land. My confession is this: I am saved and sanctified, called to preach Christ and Him crucified, ready to die or ready to live for Jesus. May God bless the reader and fill him or her with the Holy Spirit.

THE END.